AQA Biology

GCSE

Higher Workbook

Gemma Young
Editor: Lawrie Ryan

Great Clarendon Street, Oxford, OX2 6DP, United Kingdom

Oxford University Press is a department of the University of Oxford. It furthers the University's objective of excellence in research, scholarship, and education by publishing worldwide. Oxford is a registered trade mark of Oxford University Press in the UK and in certain other countries

British Library Cataloguing in Publication Data
Data available

978 0 19 842167 2

10

The manufacturing process conforms to the environmental regulations of the country of origin.

Printed and bound in Great Britain by Bell and Bain Ltd, Glasgow

Acknowledgements

Cover: ETHAN DANIELS/SCIENCE PHOTO LIBRARY

p12: JOHN DURHAM/SCIENCE PHOTO LIBRARY; **p49**: Radu Bercan/Shutterstock; **p133**: Oxford University Press; **p148**: Artur Synenko/Shutterstock.

Artwork by Q2A Media Services Ltd.

Contents

Introduction

Key content – Each topic from your GCSE Student Book is covered, and includes a summary of the key content you need to know

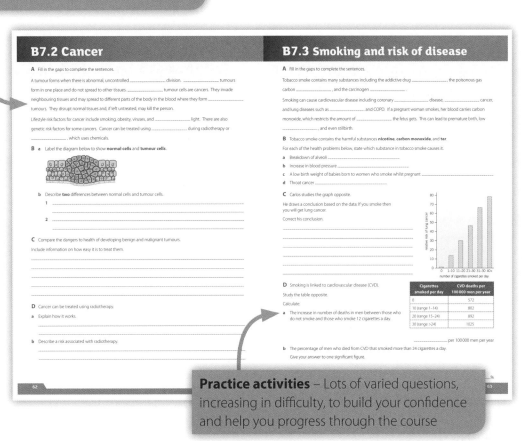

Practice activities – Lots of varied questions, increasing in difficulty, to build your confidence and help you progress through the course

Hints – Handy hints to give you extra guidance on how to answer more complex questions

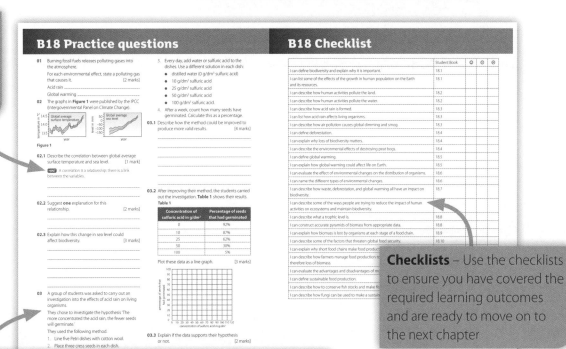

Checklists – Use the checklists to ensure you have covered the required learning outcomes and are ready to move on to the next chapter

Practice questions – Practice questions appear at the end of each chapter, to test your knowledge. They include a mix of short and long-answer question types, as well as practical-focused questions so you can practise the key skills required for your examinations. All answers are in the Workbook, allowing for instant feedback and self-assessment

B1.1 The world of the microscope

A Fill in the gaps to complete the sentences.

Microscopes can make objects look bigger – they _____ them. You need a microscope to see cells

because they are too _____ to see with just your eyes. Light microscopes use a beam of light to form

an image of an object. Electron microscopes use a beam of _____ . Electron microscopes have a

higher _____ than light microscopes. They also have a higher _____ power, which

means they show magnified objects in more detail. However, electron microscopes are much _____

than light microsopes, and are _____ expensive.

B A **light microscope** is used to magnify objects.

Match each missing label on the diagram to the correct word below.

Write **W**, **X**, **Y**, or **Z** beside each word.

slide	
objective lens	
eyepiece lens	
light	

W

X

coarse focus

stage

fine focus

Y

Z

C You can calculate the size of objects under the microscope by using the formula:

$$\text{Size of real object} = \frac{\text{size of image}}{\text{magnification}}$$

A scientist uses a magnification of ×100 000 to view a cell. The diameter of the image is 15 mm.

Calculate the diameter of the real cell in micrometres.

_____ µm

D A hospital laboratory needs to buy a new microscope.

They will use it to examine blood and count the number of white blood cells present.

Suggest which type of microscope they should buy (electron or light).

Give **two** reasons for your answer.

_____

_____

_____

_____

B1.2 Animal and plant cells

A Fill in the gaps to complete the sentences.

Animal cells contain parts that are present in plant cells as well. These are a _____, which controls

the cell; jelly-like _____; a cell _____ around the outside; mitochondria to release

_____; and ribosomes, which are where _____ are made.

Plant and algal cells also contain extra structures. These are a cell _____ made of cellulose, which

supports the cell, _____ for photosynthesis, and a permanent _____ to keep the

cell rigid.

B Most animal cells are made up of the same parts. Give the function of each part.

a Nucleus

_____

b Cell membrane

_____

c Ribosomes

_____

d Mitochondria

_____

e Cytoplasm

_____

C Label this image of an animal cell. Use the parts listed in activity **B** above.

D Plants are also made up of cells. Using these cell parts:

nucleus   chloroplast   mitochondria   cell membrane   cell wall   permanent vacuole

draw a table classifying each cell part as 'found only in animals', 'found only in plants' or 'found in both animals
and plants'.

B1.3 Eukaryotic and prokaryotic cells

A Fill in the gaps to complete the sentences.

Animal and plant cells are examples of _____ cells. They all have genetic material enclosed

in a _____ . Bacteria are all _____ cells. Their genetic material is not in a

_____ . It forms a single DNA loop. They may contain one or more extra small rings of DNA

called _____ .

B All living organisms are made up of cells. Some are made up of **eukaryotic cells**, others of **prokaryotic cells**. Describe the similarities and differences between the two types of cells.

_____

_____

_____

_____

C This diagram shows a prokaryotic cell.

Give the function of the:

a Flagella

_____

b Plasmids

_____

c Slime capsule

_____

D **Micrometre (µm)** is a unit used to measure size in biology. 1000 µm = 1 mm

a A eukaryotic cell has a length of 100 µm. Write this in mm.

_____

b An ant has a length of 1 mm. Write this in m.

_____

c Calculate how many **orders of magnitude** there are between the length of a eukaryotic cell and an ant.

_____

B1.4 Specialisation in animal cells

A Fill in the gaps to complete the sentences.

As an organism develops, cells _____ to form different types of cell. A _____ cell has

different structures to enable it to carry out a certain _____ . Examples of specialised animal cells are

_____ cells, which carry electrical impulses; _____ cells for movement; and sperm

cells, which fertilise an _____ cell.

B Name each type of specialised cell described below:

a Changes length by contracting and relaxing _____

b Contains genetic information from the female parent _____

c Has a long axon _____

C Sperm and eggs are specialised cells. Describe how sperm are adapted for their function.

_____

_____

_____

_____

D The diagram shows an example of a specialised animal cell. It has small hair-like structures called **cilia** on its
surface. These can move backwards and forwards.

cilia

Suggest one place in the human body that these cells are found.

Give a reason for your answer.

_____

_____

_____

_____

B1.5 Specialisation in plant cells

A Fill in the gaps to complete the sentences.

Plant cells may be _____ to carry out a particular function. Root hair cells are one example. They

have a large surface _____ to increase water absorption. Xylem and phloem cells are involved in

transporting substances around the plant. Xylem transports _____ and dissolved mineral ions. It is

made up of tubes strengthened with _____ . Phloem carries dissolved food. _____

plates at the ends of the cells allow this to move freely up and down the tubes.

B Like animals, plants have specialised cells – cells with particular structures to allow them to carry out a function. These special structures are called adaptations.

Here are diagrams of three specialised plant cells. Write the name of each cell under the diagrams.

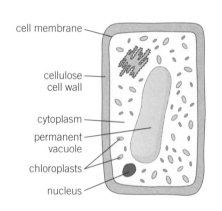

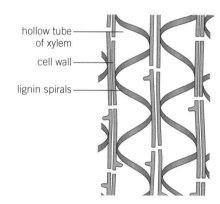

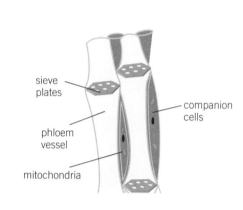

_____   _____   _____

C Complete the table to name the specialised cells of plants and explain how their adaptation helps them to perform their function.

Specialised cell	Adaptation	How this helps it to perform its function
a	Sieve plates	Allow movement of dissolved food up and down the stem
b	Rings of lignin	c

D The diagram below shows a specialised plant cell.

a Name this cell.

_____

_____

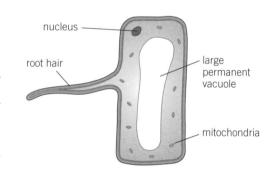

b Explain how it is adapted for its function.

_____

_____

_____

B1.6 Diffusion

A Fill in the gaps to complete the sentences.

Diffusion is the spreading out of particles, resulting in a net _____ from an area of

_____ concentration to an area of _____ concentration. The _____

of diffusion is affected by the difference in concentration (the concentration _____), the temperature,

and the available surface _____ . Substances move in and out of cells by diffusion. Examples are

glucose, urea, and gases such as _____ and carbon dioxide.

B Complete the diagram to show the progression of diffusion.

     A   B   C

C In plants, carbon dioxide diffuses from the air into the leaf.

Give **two** factors that would result in an increase in the rate of diffusion.

1 _____

2 _____

D The diagram below shows an example of a cell that lines the small intestine.

Explain how its structure helps increase the rate of diffusion of substances.

_____

_____

B1.7 Osmosis

A Fill in the gaps to complete the sentences.

Osmosis is a special type of _____ . It is the movement of _____ from a dilute

solution to a more _____ solution through a partially permeable _____ .

_____ moves into or out of a cell by osmosis if there are solutions of different concentrations inside

and outside the cell.

- If the concentration of the solution is the _____ as the concentration of the inside of the cell then

  the solution is isotonic.

- If the concentration of the solution is higher than the concentration of the inside of the cell then the solution

  is _____ .

- If the concentration of the solution is lower than the concentration of the inside of the cell then the solution

  is _____ .

B The diagram shows a particle model of water and a solute.

a Draw an arrow on the diagram to show the net movement of water molecules.

b Explain why the arrow points in this direction.

_____

_____

_____

water molecule   sugar   partially permeable membrane

C Some scientists added three different animal cells to solutions containing different concentrations of glucose.

Complete the table to show if the solutions outside of the cell are **isotonic**, **hypertonic**, or **hypotonic** compared to the solution of the inside of the cell.

Cell	Concentration of glucose inside the cell in g/dm³	Concentration of glucose in the solution outside the cell in g/dm³	What is the solution?
X	0.5	0.1	
Y	0.8	1.2	
Z	0.4	0.4	

D Describe what the scientists would see happen to cells **X** and **Y** from activity **C** above.

cell **X** _____

cell **Y** _____

E The concentration of solutes in the blood plasma is kept relatively constant.

Suggest why this is important.

_____

_____

_____

_____

B1.8 Osmosis in plants

A Fill in the gaps to complete the sentences.

Osmosis is important to maintain pressure called _____ in plant cells. This keeps the cells rigid. If a

plant cell _____ water it becomes _____ (soft). This causes the plant to wilt. If a

cell loses a lot of water the cell _____ pulls away from the cell wall. This is called _____ .

B Water enters and leaves plant cells by osmosis. The amount of water in the cell affects the structure of the cell.

a Describe how a plant cell is kept turgid.

_____

_____

Describe how a plant cell becomes:

b flaccid

_____

_____

c plasmolysed

_____

_____

C Marco investigated osmosis in potato cells.

He placed discs of potato in different concentrations of sugar solution. He then left them for 30 minutes.

He measured the percentage change in mass and plotted his results on a graph.

a Draw a line of best fit.

b One of the results is anomalous (looks wrong). Circle it.

c Complete Marco's conclusion.

– Describe what happened to the mass of the discs at each sugar concentration.

– Explain why this happened.

i At sugar solutions of 0 and 20 g/dm³

_____

_____

ii At a sugar solution of 30 g/dm³

_____

_____

iii At sugar solutions of 40 g/dm³ and above

_____

_____

B1.9 Active transport

A Fill in the gaps to complete the sentences.

Active transport moves substances from a more _____ solution to a more concentrated solution. This is against a concentration _____ .

Active transport uses energy released from food during _____ . Plant _____ hairs absorb mineral ions from very dilute solutions in the _____ using active transport. Active transport also enables sugar molecules to be absorbed from lower concentrations in the gut into the blood, where the concentration of sugar is _____ .

B **a** Describe one similarity between **active transport** and **diffusion**.

_____

_____

b Describe one difference between active transport and diffusion.

_____

_____

C **a** Describe what this graph shows.

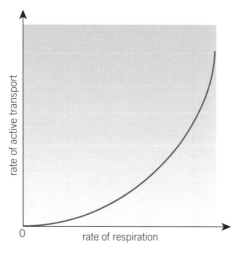

_____

_____

b Using the graph, explain why a plant will die if its roots are in soil that contains low levels of oxygen.

_____

_____

_____

B1.10 Exchanging materials

A Fill in the gaps to complete the sentences.

Single-celled organisms have a relatively _____ surface area to volume ratio. As a cell increases in

size, the surface area to volume ratio _____ .

Multicellular organisms have special surfaces where exchange of materials takes place.

Exchange surfaces usually have a _____ surface area and _____ walls, which give

short diffusion distances. Examples in plants are roots and leaves. In animals, exchange surfaces also have an efficient

_____ supply. Examples include gills in _____ and alveoli in humans.

B The surface area to volume ratio (SA : V ratio) is very important in biology.

A student measured the surface area to volume ratio of some different-sized cubes.

Complete the gaps in the table.

cube **X**

cube **Y**

2 cm   4 cm

Cube	Length of one side in cm	Area of one side in cm²	Total area of all sides in cm²	Volume in cm³	SA : V ratio
Example	1	1	6	1	6 : 1
X	2	4		8	
Y	4		96		1.5 : 1

C Multicellular organisms, like humans, require a circulatory system. However, unicellular organisms can survive
without one. Suggest why.

_____

_____

_____

D Your lungs contain millions of tiny air sacs (**alveoli**) where gas exchange takes place between the air and the blood.

The diagram shows a group of alveoli.

Describe **two** ways that alveoli are adapted for effective gas exchange.

_____

_____

_____

B1 Practice questions

01 **Figure 1** shows a leaf from a water plant called *Elodea* viewed under a light microscope.

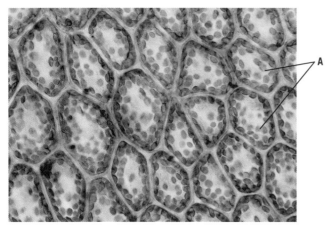

Figure 1

01.1 The cells contain many small green structures. These are labelled **A** on **Figure 1**.

Write their name.

Describe their function. [2 marks]

_____

_____

_____

01.2 An *Elodea* leaf is 10 mm long.

The length of one of the green structures is 10 μm.

Calculate the difference in order of magnitude between the length of the two structures. [3 marks]

_____

_____

_____

02 Placing plant tissue in sugar solution may cause water to enter or leave the tissue.

02.1 Name the transport process involved in the movement of water across a cell membrane. [1 mark]

_____

02.2 A group of students was asked to carry out an experiment to show how the concentration of sugar solution affects how much water enters or leaves the cell by the process identified in **02.1**.

Write a suitable method. Include the equipment they could use. [6 marks]

_____

_____

_____

_____

_____

_____

_____

_____

_____

_____

_____

_____

_____

_____

_____

_____

_____

03 **Figure 2** shows a sperm cell.

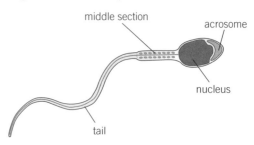

Figure 2

Explain how it is specialised to carry out its function. [3 marks]

_____

_____

_____

_____

_____

B1 Checklist

	Student Book	☺	😐	☹
I can describe how microscopy techniques have developed over time.	1.1			
I can describe the differences in magnification and resolution between a light microscope and an electron microscope.	1.1			
I can calculate the magnification, real size, and image size of a specimen.	1.1			
I can list the main parts of animal cells.	1.2			
I can describe the similarities and differences between plant and animal cells.	1.2			
I can describe the similarities and differences between eukaryotic cells and prokaryotic cells.	1.3			
I can describe how bacteria compare with animal and plant cells.	1.3			
I can describe the size and scale of cells using order of magnitude calculations.	1.3			
I can describe how cells differentiate to form specialised cells.	1.4			
I can explain how animal cells may be specialised to carry out a particular function.	1.4			
I can describe how the structure of different types of animal cells relates to their function.	1.4			
I can explain how plant cells may be specialised to carry out a particular function.	1.5			
I can describe how the structure of different types of plant cells relates to their function.	1.5			
I can describe how diffusion takes place and why it is important in living organisms.	1.6			
I can list what affects the rate of diffusion.	1.6			
I can compare and contrast osmosis and diffusion.	1.7			
I can explain why osmosis is important in animal cells.	1.7			
I can explain why osmosis is important in plant cells.	1.8			
I can describe an investigation into the effect of osmosis on plant tissues.	1.8			
I can describe how active transport works.	1.9			
I can explain the importance of active transport in cells.	1.9			
I can describe how the surface area to volume ratio varies depending on the size of an organism.	1.10			
I can explain why large multicellular organisms need special systems for exchanging materials with the environment.	1.10			

B2.1 Cell division

A Fill in the gaps to complete the sentences.

Body cells divide in a series of stages called the cell _____ . During the cell cycle the genetic material

is doubled. One set of chromosomes is pulled to each end of the cell. The nucleus divides into _____

identical nuclei in a process called _____ . Finally the cytoplasm and cell membranes divide to form two

identical cells.

Mitotic cell division is important in the growth, _____ , and development of multicellular organisms.

B Genetic material is found in your cells.

Define the following terms:

a DNA

_____

b Gene

_____

c Chromosome

_____

d Nucleus

_____

C A body cell from a wallaby contains 10 **chromosomes**, arranged in pairs.

a Why do its body cells contain chromosomes arranged in *pairs*?

_____

b The diagram shows a cell undergoing the two stages of **cell division**.

Write the total number of chromosomes in the nucleus of each of the cells after each division.

D In a discussion about the **cell cycle**, one student suggests 'During mitosis the DNA replicates, the nucleus divides
and then the cell splits into two'.

Correct this statement.

_____

_____

_____

B2.2 Growth and differentiation

A Fill in the gaps to complete the sentences.

Stem cells are unspecialised and have the ability to _____ into many different types of cell.

In animals they are found in _____ and in some places in adults.

In plant cells, new unspecialised cells are formed in the _____ found in the shoot and

_____ tips. They then differentiate. This process takes place throughout the plant's life.

B Describe what **differentiation** is.

Explain why it is important.

_____

_____

_____

C a Give **two** ways that differentiation is the same in plants and animals.

_____

_____

_____

_____

b Give **two** ways that differentiation is different in plants and animals.

_____

_____

_____

_____

D Describe where areas containing stem cells are found in plants.

_____

B2.3 Stem cells

A Fill in the gaps to complete the sentences.

Embryonic and _____ stem cells can be cloned and made to differentiate into many different types of

cell. Treatment with stem cells may be able to help conditions such as paralysis and _____ .

Stem cells from plant _____ are used to produce new plant clones. They can be grown

_____ and cheaply and are used for research and farming.

B Name the following:

a **one** medical condition that could be cured by stem cells.

1 _____

b **two** types of human stem cells.

1 _____

2 _____

c **three** places in the adult human body where stem cells are found.

1 _____

2 _____

3 _____

C You can take a cutting of a plant and use it to produce a whole new plant which is identical to the original plant. The diagram below shows how.

Suggest why:

a In step 2 just the tip of the plant is removed.

_____

_____

b In step 3 the tip of the plant is dipped into a powder that promotes differentiation of stem cells.

_____

_____

c A polythene bag is used to cover the plant in step 4.

_____

_____

B2.4 Stem cell dilemmas

A Fill in the gaps to complete the sentences.

The use of embryonic stem cells in medicine has potential benefits but also has some _____ as well as

_____ , social, and economic issues. In _____ cloning, an embryo is produced with the

same genes as the patient. The patient does not _____ the stem cells so they may be used for a medical

treatment. Scientists are also researching ways of using _____ stem cells in medicine.

B Scientists are researching the use of embryonic stem cells to cure some diseases. The diagram opposite shows how this works.

Write the letters for the statements below in the correct boxes to label the diagram.

V The stem cells are made to differentiate into different types of specialised cell.

W The stem cells are cloned.

X An early human embryo is grown in a dish.

Y Tissues or organs made up of specialised cells are transplanted into the patient.

Z Stem cells are removed from the embryo.

spinal cord   heart   kidney   insulin-producing cells

C Using human **stem cells** for medical treatments is a new technology. There are issues associated with it.

Read the following information.

Stem cells are taken from embryos. The embryos will be destroyed after being used.

Stem cells divide and grow quickly. There is some concern that embryonic stem cells might cause cancer if they are used to treat people.

Some research has proven the potential of stem cells to treat conditions such as paralysis and diabetes.

However, progress in developing these therapies has been relatively slow, difficult, and expensive. Some people feel that this money would be better spent on research into other areas of medicine.

Evaluate the use of stem cells for medical treatments.

You should mention the benefits, risks, and any ethical or economical concerns.

Remember to include a justified conclusion.

_____

_____

_____

_____

_____

_____

_____

B2 Practice questions

01 **Figure 1** shows one way in which scientists hope embryonic stem cells might be used in medical treatments in the future.

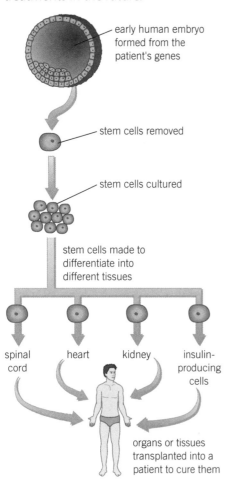

early human embryo formed from the patient's genes

stem cells removed

stem cells cultured

stem cells made to differentiate into different tissues

spinal cord heart kidney insulin-producing cells

organs or tissues transplanted into a patient to cure them

Figure 1

01.1 What is the name of this medical treatment?
[1 mark]

_____

01.2 Name **one** condition that could be treated in this way. [1 mark]

_____

01.3 Give **two** reasons why embryonic stem cells are used for this treatment. [2 marks]

1 _____

2 _____

01.4 Explain one ethical objection some people have with this treatment. [2 marks]

_____

_____

02 **Figure 2** shows the cell cycle. There are 3 stages.

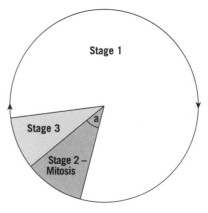

Stage 1

Stage 3

a

Stage 2 – Mitosis

Figure 2

02.1 Describe **one** function of the cell cycle. [1 mark]

_____

_____

02.2 Identify the stage at which the following take place: [1 mark]

The nucleus divides _____

The DNA is copied _____

The cell splits into two _____

02.3 The original cell had 48 **pairs** of chromosomes.

What is the **total number** of chromosomes in each of the new cells produced by the cell cycle? [1 mark]

_____

02.4 The total length of the cell cycle is 20 hours.

In **Figure 2**, angle a = 37°.

Calculate the length of mitosis to one significant figure. [2 marks]

_____ hours

03 Cloning is the production of an identical copy of an individual.

An adult plant can be cloned by taking stem or root tissue.

Explain why it is simple to clone an adult plant but not an adult animal. [4 marks]

_____

_____

_____

_____

_____

B2 Checklist

	Student Book	☺	😐	☹
I can describe the role of the chromosomes in cells.	2.1			
I can explain the importance of the cell cycle.	2.1			
I can describe how cells divide by mitosis.	2.1			
I can compare and contrast cell differentiation in animals and plants.	2.2			
I can describe how plant clones are produced and their uses.	2.2			
I can compare stem cells to other body cells.	2.3			
I can describe the functions of stem cells in embryos, in adult animals, and in plants.	2.3			
I can describe how treatment with stem cells may be used to treat people with different medical conditions.	2.3			
I can describe the process of therapeutic cloning.	2.4			
I can evaluate some of the potential benefits, risks, and social and ethical issues of the use of stem cells in medical research and treatments.	2.4			

B3.1 Tissues and organs

A Fill in the gaps to complete the sentences.

A tissue is a group of _____ with similar structures and functions. An example is _____

tissue, which can contract to bring about movement. Organs are collections of _____ performing

specific functions. The _____ is an organ involved in the digestion of food. It is made up of muscular,

epithelial, and _____ tissue. Organs are organised into organ _____ , which work together

to form organisms. The stomach is part of the _____ system.

B Explain how cells are organised in the human body.

Include the words: tissues, organs, and organ systems.

_____

_____

_____

C The stomach is an **organ** made up of several different **tissues**. Use the functions given below to name each stomach tissue.

a Helps churn the food and digestive juices together _____

b Covers the inside and outside of the organ _____

c Produces digestive juices that break down food _____

D a Name each organ system described below:

   i Transport system to carry nutrients, oxygen, and carbon dioxide around the body.

   _____

   ii System to remove waste products from the body.

   _____

   iii System that facilitates the diffusion of oxygen into the bloodstream, and carbon dioxide out of the bloodstream.

   _____

   b Describe the function of the digestive system.

   _____

   _____

B3.2 The human digestive system

A Fill in the gaps to complete the sentences.

The _____ system in a mammal is an organ system where several _____ work together

to digest and absorb food. During digestion large _____ food molecules are broken down into

_____ soluble molecules that can enter the _____ .

B Label the diagram of the human digestive system.

pancreas

rectum

anus

C a Name three glands that produce digestive enzymes.

_____

b Describe how the stomach helps in the digestion of food.

_____

_____

c The small intestine is long, and has a good blood supply and a large surface area.
Explain the function of these three features.

_____

_____

_____

_____

B3.3 The chemistry of food

A Fill in the gaps to complete the sentences.

Carbohydrates, _____ , and lipids are food molecules. They are made up of smaller molecules joined together. Simple sugars are carbohydrates that contain only one or two sugar units. Complex carbohydrates, such as _____ , contain long chains of simple sugar units bonded together. Lipids consist of three molecules of fatty acids bonded to a molecule of _____ . Protein molecules are made up of long chains of _____ acids.

B Complete the table to show information about carbohydrates, lipids, and proteins.

Food molecule	One food that is a good source	Use in the body	Molecules formed during digestion
Carbohydrates			
Lipids			
Proteins			

C Hormone receptor molecules on the surface of cell membranes are protein molecules.

The hormone fits into the receptor and triggers a response in the cell.

a Explain why the shape of the receptor is important to its function.

_____

_____

_____

b Suggest why the cell response to the hormone will not be triggered if the pH of the surroundings changes.

_____

_____

_____

D You have been given a packet of dry soup.

Describe the food tests you would carry out to find out if the soup contains **starch**, **protein**, and **glucose**. You should include the reagents you would use plus the result if the test is positive.

_____

_____

_____

_____

_____

_____

_____

_____

B3.4 Catalysts and enzymes

A Fill in the gaps to complete the sentences.

Enzymes are biological _____ . They increase the _____ of chemical reactions inside living

organisms. Enzymes are proteins. The _____ acid chains are folded to form the _____

site, which matches the shape of a specific _____ molecule. This is called the lock and _____

theory. Enzymes control _____ , the sum of all the reactions in a cell or the body. They speed up

reactions, such as building large molecules from _____ ones, _____ down large molecules,

and changing one molecule into another.

B Enzymes are biological catalysts.

Define a catalyst.

_____

_____

C Some **enzymes** are used to break up large molecules.

The diagram shows this.

Explain what is taking place in each step (labelled 1–3) in
the diagram.

Use the terms: **enzyme, substrate, active site, product**

_____

_____

_____

_____

_____

D A student wanted to find out which catalyst, manganese(IV) oxide or an enzyme called catalase, would break
down hydrogen peroxide at the fastest rate.

They have a stopwatch and the equipment shown opposite.

Describe how they should carry out the investigation. Include the
control variables in your answer.

rubber tubing

gas
syringe

hydrogen peroxide solution
and catalyst

_____

_____

_____

_____

_____

_____

_____

_____

_____

B3.5 Factors affecting enzyme action

A Fill in the gaps to complete the sentences.

Enzyme activity is affected by _____ and pH. The temperature that an enzyme works fastest at is

called its _____ temperature. High temperatures and changes in pH _____ the enzyme,

changing the shape of the _____ site. This means that the _____ can no longer bind to the

enzyme. Different enzymes work best at different temperatures and pH levels.

B Some students are carrying out an investigation into the factors that affect enzyme action.

They mix 2 g of albumin protein with 100 cm³ of pure water.

They notice that the mixture is cloudy because of the insoluble albumin protein.

They then place 25 cm³ of this mixture into a test tube and add 1 cm³ of protease enzyme.

They decide to investigate how the temperature affects the rate of the reaction.

a Plan how they should carry out this investigation.

_____

_____

_____

_____

_____

_____

b Give **two** other variables that will affect the rate of this reaction.

1 _____

2 _____

c The students plot a graph of their results.

For each temperature range given below:

Describe the trend.

Give an explanation for the trend.

i   0–35 °C

Trend: _____

Explanation: _____

_____

ii   35–41 °C

Trend: _____

Explanation: _____

_____

iii   41–54 °C

Trend: _____

Explanation: _____

_____

B3.6 How the digestive system works

A Fill in the gaps to complete the sentences.

Digestive enzymes are produced by specialised cells in _____ and in the lining of the digestive

system. The enzymes are released from the cells into the digestive system where they mix with food. The enzymes

catalyse the breakdown of large, _____ food molecules into smaller, soluble molecules that can be

absorbed into the bloodstream. _____ such as amylase catalyse the breakdown of carbohydrates to

simple sugars. Proteases catalyse the breakdown of _____ to amino acids. _____ catalyse

the breakdown of _____ to fatty acids and glycerol.

B Digestive enzymes are released by **glands** in the body. They catalyse the breakdown of food molecules.

Complete the table to show what **substrates** they work on and where in the body they are produced.

Enzyme	Substrate	Where in the body the enzyme is produced
amylase		1. mouth (salivary glands)
		2.
	protein	1.
		2. pancreas
		3.
lipase		1.
		2. small intestine

C A group of students carried out an investigation into how pH affects the activity of amylase.

This is the method they followed:

1 Add 10 cm³ of starch solution to a boiling tube.

2 Add a few drops of hydrochloric acid until the pH of the starch solution is 2.

3 Mix in 1 cm³ of amylase.

4 Every 30 seconds, take a few drops of the mixture and add it to some iodine.

5 Time how long it takes before the iodine no longer changes colour to blue/black.

6 Repeat for pHs of 5, 7, 9, and 12.

a Which step from 1 to 5 will need to change in each test? _____

b Describe how the students should use the results to find out the optimum pH of amylase.

_____

_____

c On carrying out the method, the students found that for every pH tested, the iodine did not change colour, even after 10 minutes. Suggest a probable reason for this, and what they can do to resolve this problem.

_____

_____

_____

_____

D People who suffer from cystic fibrosis produce thick mucus which clogs up the pancreas, preventing pancreatic juices from reaching the small intestine.

Suggest what effect this has on the growth of a child with cystic fibrosis. Give a reason for your answer.

_____

_____

_____

_____

B3.7 Making digestion efficient

A Fill in the gaps to complete the sentences.

Protease enzymes in the stomach work best in acidic conditions. The stomach produces hydrochloric

_____ , which maintains a _____ pH. The enzymes made in the pancreas and the small

intestine work best in _____ conditions. Bile is produced by the _____ and stored

in the _____ . It is released along the bile _____ into the duodenum. It has an alkaline

pH to _____ stomach acid. Bile also breaks down large fat globules into _____ droplets.

This is called emulsifying.

B A students says 'bile breaks down lipids into fatty acids and glycerol'.

Explain why the student is incorrect.

Give a correct description of the function of bile.

_____

_____

_____

C

Use the information in the graph to explain why **bile** has an important role in the digestion of **starch**.

_____

_____

_____

_____

B3 Practice questions

01 **Figure 1** shows some organs in the digestive system.

01.1 Use the words below to label **Figure 1**.

liver **pancreas** **gall bladder**

Figure 1

[1 mark]

01.2 Describe the role of the liver and gall bladder in digestion. [2 marks]

Liver _____

_____

Gall bladder _____

_____

02 A student investigated the effect of bile on lipase.

- They set up two test tubes containing: lipase and sunflower oil; lipase, sunflower oil, and bile.

- They added a few drops of phenolphthalein. This is an indicator that is pink at alkaline pHs but goes colourless in acidic pHs.

- They placed each test tube into a water bath at 37 °C.

- They timed how long it took for the phenolphthalein in each tube to go colourless.

- They repeated the experiment twice.

The results are shown in **Table 1**.

Table 1

Test tube	Time taken for phenolphthalein to go colourless in seconds			
	1	2	3	Mean
Lipase and oil	124	120	122	122
Lipase, oil, and bile	91	139	88	

02.1 Calculate the value for the mean time taken for phenolphthalein to go colourless in the test tube containing lipase, oil, and bile.

Show your working below. [2 marks]

_____

02.2 Explain why the phenolphthalein went colourless. [2 marks]

_____

_____

02.3 Describe what the results show.

Give a reason for this. [4 marks]

_____

_____

_____

_____

_____

02.4 Describe what the student could do to check the reproducibility of their results. [2 marks]

_____

_____

_____

B3 Checklist

	Student Book	☺	😐	☹
I can describe how specialised cells become organised into tissues.	3.1			
I can describe how several different tissues work together to form an organ.	3.1			
I can identify the main organs of the human digestive system.	3.2			
I can describe the basic structures of carbohydrates, proteins, and lipids.	3.3			
I can define what a catalyst is.	3.4			
I can describe enzymes as biological catalysts.	3.4			
I can describe what the metabolism of the body involves.	3.4			
I can explain how temperature and pH affect enzyme action.	3.5			
I can describe enzymes as working fastest at different temperatures and pH values.	3.5			
I can describe how the food I eat is digested in my body.	3.6			
I can describe the roles played by the different digestive enzymes.	3.6			
I can describe how hydrochloric acid and bile make digestion more efficient.	3.7			

B4.1 The blood

A Fill in the gaps to complete the sentences.

The blood, _____ , and blood vessels make up the human circulatory system. _____

is a liquid that has blood cells suspended in it and transports other substances around the body. Red blood cells

contain a red pigment called _____ that binds to oxygen to transport it from the _____ to

body cells. White blood cells help to protect the body against infection with _____ . Platelets are cell

fragments that start the _____ process at wound sites.

B Your **blood** is a tissue made up of a several parts.

Complete the table to show the names of these parts and their functions.

Part of blood	Function
	Transports all of the blood cells and other substances around the body
Red blood cells	
	Forms part of the body's defence system against harmful microorganisms
Platelets	

C If a person loses a lot of blood in an accident they may be given a blood transfusion.

Blood from a donor is transferred to their body to replace the blood they have lost.

There are risks associated with a blood transfusion.

Suggest one risk and explain how it can be minimised.

_____

_____

_____

_____

_____

D Red blood cells are specialised cells.

For each of the adaptations below, explain how it makes red blood cells efficient at their function.

a They contain the red pigment **haemoglobin**.

_____

_____

b They have no nucleus.

_____

_____

c They are biconcave discs (pushed in on both sides).

_____

_____

d They are very flexible.

_____

_____

A Fill in the gaps to complete the sentences.

Blood flows around the body in the blood vessels. The main types of blood vessel are arteries, _____ , and

capillaries. Substances diffuse in and out of the blood in the _____ .

Veins have _____ . These prevent backflow, ensuring that blood flows in the right direction. _____

and other mammals have a _____ circulatory system. This contains two separate transport systems. One

carries blood from the heart to the _____ to exchange gases. The other carries blood from the heart to all

organs in the body and back again.

B There are three main types of blood vessel: arteries, capillaries, and veins.

Label the diagrams with the name of each blood vessel.

thick walls   small lumen

thick layer of muscle and elastic fibres

relatively thin walls   large lumen

often have valves

walls a single cell thick   tiny vessel with narrow lumen

C In fish the blood travels through the heart and to the gills. It then travels around the rest of the body before returning to the heart. The cycle is repeated.

a Explain why the blood travels to the gills.

_____

_____

b Do fish have a **double circulatory system**?

Give a reason for your answer.

_____

_____

D The diagram shows a double circulatory system.

For each letter, say what type of blood vessel is being shown.

U _____   X _____

V _____   Y _____

W _____   Z _____

B4.3 The heart

A Fill in the gaps to complete the sentences.

It is an organ that pumps _____ around the body. It contains _____ sides, each with

chambers called an atrium and a _____ . The right side pumps blood to the _____ . The

_____ side pumps blood all around the body. Heart _____ keep the blood flowing in the

right direction.

Coronary heart disease is caused by narrow or blocked arteries that supply the heart muscle with

_____ . Treatments include _____ , bypass surgery, and drugs called _____ .

B Name the blood vessel of the heart that carries:

a Oxygenated blood from the lungs to the heart. _____

b Deoxygenated blood from the heart to the lungs. _____

c Deoxygenated blood to the heart. _____

d Oxygenated blood from the heart to other blood vessels in the body. _____

C Use the diagram to help you describe the passage of blood through the heart.

Remember, blood moves through each side of the heart simultaneously. The first sentence has been written for you.

The blood is in the veins. _____

_____

_____

_____

_____

D The blood vessels that supply blood to the heart are called **coronary arteries**. If blood flow through them is
reduced, it can cause pain or a heart attack.

Complete the sentences to describe the different ways to treat this problem.

The coronary arteries can be widened by using a _____ .

An alternative route for the blood can be provided by carrying out _____ .

The risk of heart disease can be reduced by taking drugs called _____ .

B4.4 Helping the heart

A Fill in the gaps to complete the sentences.

Damaged heart valves can be replaced using biological or _____ valves. Biological valves are taken from _____ or human donors.

The resting heart rate of around 70 beats per minute is controlled by a group of cells in the right _____ . This is called the _____ .

_____ pacemakers are electrical devices used to correct irregularities in the heart rhythm.

If a person's heart fails they can have a transplant. _____ hearts are occasionally used to keep patients alive while they wait for a transplant. They are also used to give a diseased heart a rest to help it recover.

B A faulty heart valve can be replaced with either a **mechanical valve** or a **biological valve**.

The table below shows more information on each type.

Type of valve	Material	How long they last	Other issues
Mechanical	Titanium and polymers	20–25 years	Patient will need to take drugs to stop clots forming
Biological	Animal tissue	12–15 years	The valves are taken from animal (cow or pig) or human donors

a Explain the economic issues associated with both valves.

_____
_____
_____
_____

b Suggest why a person's personal beliefs might dictate which type of valve they have.

_____
_____

c Evaluate the benefits and risks to the patient that are associated with having a faulty valve replaced.

_____
_____
_____
_____

C When a person's heart fails completely they can have a **heart transplant**. The heart comes from a person who has died and donated their heart.

Explain why it is common to wait a long time for a heart transplant.

_____
_____
_____

B4.5 Breathing and gas exchange

A Fill in the gaps to complete the sentences.

The lungs are in your chest cavity, protected by your _____ and separated from your abdomen by

a sheet of muscle called the _____ . During breathing in, air travels down the _____

and into smaller and smaller tubes that end in air sacs called alveoli. The alveoli provide a very large surface

_____ and a rich supply of blood _____ . This means gases can diffuse into and out of the

blood as efficiently as possible. During gas exchange, _____ passes from the alveoli into the blood and

carbon dioxide passes from the _____ into the alveoli.

B Use the words below to label the diagram of the human gas exchange system.

alveoli   **bronchi**   **bronchiole**   **lungs**   **trachea**

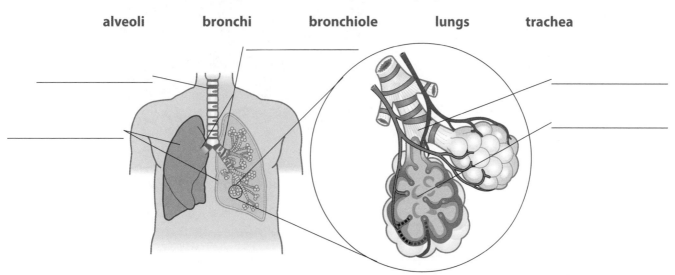

C Exchange of gases between the air and the blood takes place in the **alveoli**. This means that the percentage of
some gases changes between the air you breathe in and the air you breathe out.

Complete the table by writing in the correct percentages for each gas.

Gas	% in air breathed in	% in air breathed out
carbon dioxide	0.04	
nitrogen	80	
oxygen		16

D **Exchange surfaces** have a number of adaptations so exchange can take place efficiently.

Relate each adaptation listed below to the structure of the alveoli.

a Good blood supply

_____

b Large surface area

_____

c Steep concentration gradient

_____

d Short distance for diffusion

_____

B4.6 Tissues and organs in plants

A Fill in the gaps to complete the sentences.

Plant organs include the flowers, stem, leaves, and _____ . They are made up of several different

tissues. The function of the leaf is to carry out _____ . One example of a tissue in the leaf is the lower

_____ . It contains holes called _____ , which allow gases to enter and leave the leaf. The

roots, _____ , and leaves form a plant organ system for the transport of substances around the plant.

B Use the words below to label the diagram of a leaf cross-section.

vascular bundle

stomata

upper epidermis

palisade mesophyll

guard cell

air space

spongy mesophyll

lower epidermis

C The function of the leaf is to carry out photosynthesis.

Explain how the different tissues labelled in the diagram in activity **B** work together to carry out this function.

_____

_____

_____

_____

_____

_____

D The stem of a sunflower plant is 1 m long.

An individual cell in the stem has a length of 100 μm.

Calculate how many orders of magnitude there are between the length of the cell and the length of the stem.

_____

B4.7 Transport systems in plants

A Fill in the gaps to complete the sentences.

Plants have separate transport systems.

_____ tissue transports water and mineral ions from the _____ to the stems and leaves. Sugar is made in the _____ during photosynthesis. _____ tissue transports dissolved sugars from the leaves to the rest of the plant, including the growing regions and storage organs.

Plants need sugars to release _____ via respiration. They also use them for growth. Mineral ions are used to make _____ . Water is needed for photosynthesis as well as keeping the cells rigid so the plant is supported.

B Where are the following substances transported (from and to) in a plant and through which vessels?

Water _____

Mineral ions _____

Sugars _____

C a What is the movement of dissolved sugars around a plant called?

_____

b Describe its role in the plant.

_____

_____

_____

D A student places a stick of celery into a glass containing water dyed with blue food colouring.

He leaves it for 24 hours.

He then slices the stem to reveal a cross-section.

a Predict what he will observe.

_____

b Give a reason for this observation.

_____

_____

_____

B4.8 Evaporation and transpiration

A Fill in the gaps to complete the sentences.

The loss of water vapour from the surface of plant leaves is known as _____ . Water is lost through tiny

holes in the underside of the _____ called stomata. The _____ cells control their opening

and closing.

Stomata open to let _____ in for photosynthesis. At the same time, _____ vapour can

evaporate from the leaves. This causes more water to be pulled up through the _____ tubes to take

its place.

B Plants need to exchange gases with the air for photosynthesis.

Tick the boxes in the table opposite to show the direction of net diffusion of gases in and out of the leaf.

Substance	✓ if diffused into the leaf	✓ if diffused out of the leaf
water vapour		
oxygen		
carbon dioxide		

C Water moves in one direction through a plant.

Use the diagram below to help you describe how.

_____

_____

_____

_____

_____

D A student views the underside of a leaf using a microscope. The image opposite shows what they see.

The area of the field of view is 0.05 mm^2.

Estimate how many stomata would be found in the whole underside of the leaf (area of 70 mm^2).

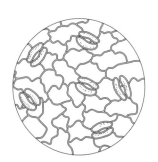

_____

B4.9 Factors affecting transpiration

A Fill in the gaps to complete the sentences.

Factors that _____ the rate of photosynthesis will increase the rate of transpiration. This is because

more stomata will be open to let _____ into the leaf. When stomata are open, _____

_____ is lost by evaporation. Therefore, an increase in _____ intensity will increase the rate

of transpiration.

Also, factors that affect the evaporation rate will affect the rate of transpiration. These factors include

_____ , humidity, and air flow. The rate of transpiration can be measured using equipment called a

_____ . Transpiration is _____ in hot, dry, windy, or bright conditions.

B This equipment is used to measure the rate of transpiration. What is it called?

leafy shoot

water

reservoir

capillary tube filled with water

air bubble

scale

_____

C A student used to equipment in activity **B** to study the effect of light intensity and wind on the rate of transpiration.
They used a fan to make the air windy.

a Suggest how they can change the light intensity.

_____

b They used still air and a light intensity of 50 units.
The air bubble moved 2.4 cm in 4 minutes.
Calculate the rate of transpiration in **mm/min.**

_____ mm/min

rate of transpiration

light intensity

X = windy
Y = still air

c They drew a graph of their results.
Give **two** conclusions that can be drawn from the graph.

1 _____

_____

2 _____

_____

B4 Practice questions

01 **Figure 1** shows a cross-section of a blood vessel. It is based on an image taken using a light microscope.

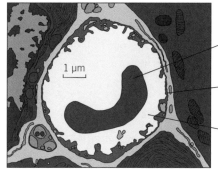

Figure 1

01.1 What type of blood vessel is shown in **Figure 1**?

[1 mark]

_____

01.2 Explain how you decided your answer [1 mark]

_____

_____

01.3 A scientist used a light microscope to measure the rate flow of red blood cells through the blood vessel.

They observed that a red blood cell travelled 1 mm in 1.4 seconds.

Calculate the rate of flow of the red blood cell. Include the correct unit. [2 marks]

_____

02 The coronary arteries supply the heart tissue with blood.

They can become narrow because of a build-up of fatty material on the lining of the vessels.

02.1 Explain how this narrowing affects the heart.

[4 marks]

_____

_____

_____

_____

02.2 There are two different treatments available for the narrowing: a stent or heart bypass surgery.

a Describe how each treatment is carried out.

[4 marks]

_____

_____

_____

_____

_____

_____

_____

_____

_____

b Evaluate the risks and benefits of each treatment. [6 marks]

_____

_____

_____

_____

_____

_____

_____

_____

_____

_____

_____

_____

_____

_____

B4 Checklist

	Student Book	☺	☻	☹
I can describe how substances are transported to and from cells.	4.1			
I can name the different components in the blood.	4.1			
I can give the functions of each main component of the blood.	4.1			
I can describe how the blood flows around the body.	4.2			
I can name the different types of blood vessel.	4.2			
I can describe why valves are important.	4.2			
I can explain the importance of a double circulatory system.	4.2			
I can describe the structure and functions of the heart.	4.3			
I can describe ways of solving problems with the blood supply to the heart and problems with valves.	4.3			
I can describe how the heart keeps its natural rhythm.	4.4			
I can explain how artificial pacemakers work.	4.4			
I can describe what artificial hearts can do.	4.4			
I can identify parts of the human gas exchange system.	4.5			
I can describe how gases are exchanged in the alveoli of the lungs.	4.5			
I can describe the roles of organs in the plant organ system for the transport of substances around the plant.	4.6			
I can name the substances that are transported in plants.	4.7			
I can describe how transport in the xylem tissue differs from transport in the phloem tissue.	4.7			
I can describe what transpiration is.	4.8			
I can describe the role of stomata and guard cells in controlling gas exchange and water loss.	4.8			
I can name the factors that affect the rate of transpiration.	4.9			
I can suggest ways of investigating the effect of environmental factors on rates of water uptake in the plant.	4.9			

B5.1 Health and disease

A Fill in the gaps to complete the sentences.

Health is a state of physical and _____ well-being. Diseases are major causes of ill-health. Some are

communicable. This means they are _____ and can pass from person to person. They are caused by

_____ , for example, bacteria and viruses. Other diseases are _____ . An example is

arthritis. Other factors, including food eaten (_____), stress, and life situations may have an effect on both

mental and physical health. Different types of disease may and often do interact.

B Diseases can be **communicable** (infectious) or **non-communicable**.

Name the diseases being described below:

a Common viral communicable disease spread via the air by coughing and sneezing.

_____

b Non-communicable disease that causes the airways to narrow; common in children.

_____

c Non-communicable disease caused by the body becoming resistant to the hormone insulin.

_____

C Many different factors can affect health. Complete the table to explain how each factor causes the disease.

The first one has been done for you.

Disease	Factor	Explanation
lung cancer	smoking	tar in the cigarette smoke is a cancer-causing chemical (a carcinogen)
obesity	diet	
HIV/AIDS	drug use	
diarrhoea-linked diseases	poor water quality	

D a A group of scientists investigated a hypothesis: 'The more children a person has, the more likely the person is to suffer from stress.'

They collected data from 100 adults. They asked them how many children they had and how stressed they felt on an average day, as a score out of 10.

Draw a line on the graph axes to show the trend in data they should see if their hypothesis is correct.

b Suggest how they could improve the quality of their data.

_____

_____

_____

_____

_____

stress score

number of children

B5.2 Pathogens and disease

A Fill in the gaps to complete the sentences.

Communicable diseases are caused by _____ called pathogens, which include bacteria,

_____ , fungi, and protists. Bacteria and viruses reproduce rapidly inside your body. Bacteria can

damage cells or produce _____ that make you feel ill. _____ live and reproduce inside

your cells, causing cell damage. Pathogens can be spread by direct contact, by _____ , or by water.

B Communicable diseases are caused by **microorganisms (pathogens)**, like **viruses** and **bacteria**.

Give **two** differences between viruses and bacteria.

1 _____

_____

2 _____

_____

C Viruses cause disease by destroying cells.

Describe why they destroy cells.

_____

_____

_____

_____

D Sunil has a sore throat caused by bacteria.

Explain why he has each of these symptoms:

a A high temperature

_____

_____

b His throat feels sore

_____

_____

E Complete the table to show how some communicable diseases are spread.

Disease	How it is spread
Common cold	
HIV/AIDS	
Cholera	

B5.3 Growing bacteria in the lab

A Fill in the gaps to complete the sentences.

Uncontaminated cultures of microorganisms are needed for investigating the action of chemicals such as

disinfectants and _____.

They can be grown using sterilised _____ dishes and _____ gel.

The gel contains a _____ medium, which contains nutrients that the bacteria need to grow.

When preparing a plate, you sterilise the _____ loop before use and fix the lid of the dish to prevent

unwanted _____ getting in.

Cultures should be incubated at a maximum temperature of _____ °C in schools and colleges to reduce
the likelihood of pathogens growing that might be harmful to humans.

B Describe the function of each of these pieces of equipment used when growing bacteria in the lab.

a Petri dish _____

b Culture medium _____

c Inoculating loop _____

d Incubation oven _____

C It is important to follow aseptic technique. This ensures that no contaminating bacteria grow on the culture plate.

Describe how aseptic technique is carried out at each of the stages below:

a Preparation of agar dishes

_____

_____

_____

b Inoculation of agar

_____

_____

_____

c Preparation of plates for incubation

_____

_____

D Explain why:

a in schools, cultures are incubated at a maximum temperature of 25 °C.

_____

b in industry, cultures are often incubated at temperatures of around 37 °C.

_____

B5.4 Preventing bacterial growth

A Fill in the gaps to complete the sentences.

Bacteria multiply by simple cell _____ (binary fission) as often as every 20 minutes if they have enough

_____ and a suitable temperature.

Chemicals can be used to prevent the growth of bacteria. Disinfectants are used on the environment around us.

_____ can be used on human skin. _____ can be used inside our bodies.

You can investigate the effects of disinfectants and antibiotics on bacterial growth using agar plates. These chemicals

prevent the bacteria growing and form clear areas of agar called zones of _____ . The _____
the clear area, the more effective the chemical.

B There are 10 bacteria. The mean division time for a population of bacteria is 20 minutes.

a Calculate how many times the bacteria will divide in 4 hours.

_____

b Calculate how many bacteria there will be after 4 hours.

Use your answer from part **a** and the formula below:

bacteria at the end of growth period = bacteria at the start of the growth period $\times 2^{\text{number of divisions}}$

_____

C A Petri dish containing nutrient agar is inoculated with bacteria. The plate is incubated in a warm temperature.

This graph shows the number of bacteria over time.

a Use the graph to estimate the mean division time of
the bacteria.

_____

b Predict if the growth would continue at this rate
forever. Give a reason for your answer.

_____

_____

_____

_____

B5.5 Preventing infections

A Fill in the gaps to complete the sentences.

The work of many different scientists helped prove that communicable diseases are caused by _____ . The _____ of disease can be prevented in many ways.

Simple hygiene measures include hand _____ , sneezing into a tissue, using disinfectants, destroying _____ that carry the pathogen, isolating infected individuals, and vaccination.

B Ignaz Semmelweis was a scientist in the mid-1850s. He worked in a hospital were women had their babies. He carried out a scientific investigation that helped develop the theory that infectious diseases were caused by microorganisms. Name each stage of his investigation using the terms below:

hypothesis   **method**   **conclusion**   **observation**   **results**

The pregnant women delivered by doctors rather than midwives were much more likely to die of a fever

_____

Doctors are carrying the cause of disease on their hands

_____

Make doctors wash their hands

_____

The number of deaths decreased

_____

The hypothesis is correct, but the infectious agent is not known

_____

C Name the piece of equipment that helped scientists to prove that infectious diseases are caused by microorganisms. Explain how it helped.

_____

_____

_____

D There are many ways of preventing the spread of a communicable disease.

For each disease below, give a practical way we can prevent them spreading.

Common cold

_____

Salmonella (food poisoning)

_____

B5.6 Viral diseases

A Fill in the gaps to complete the sentences.

The _____ virus is spread by drops in the air. It causes fever and a rash, and can kill. There is no cure but

there is a _____ , which has reduced the number of cases in the UK.

HIV attacks the body's _____ cells. It can be treated with antiviral drugs. If it is not treated then

_____ occurs. This means that the body's immune system has become so badly damaged it can no

longer deal with other infections or cancers. HIV is spread by the exchange of body fluids, such as _____

or breast milk.

Tobacco _____ virus (TMV) is spread by contact and insect _____ . It damages leaves and

reduces _____ so the plant can no longer make its own food. There is no treatment. Spread is prevented

by field hygiene and pest control.

B HIV can cause the illness AIDS.

a Describe **two** ways that the HIV virus is spread.

1 _____

2 _____

b Describe **two** ways that its spread can be reduced.

1 _____

2 _____

C The graph below shows the number of people infected with measles over a number of years.

a Describe the general trend from 1965.

_____

_____

_____

_____

b Suggest a reason for this trend.

_____

_____

D A farmer is growing tomato plants inside a large greenhouse. He notices that some of his plants in one corner of the greenhouse have become infected with tobacco mosaic virus.

a Explain why this disease will kill the plant.

_____

_____

b Suggest what he should do to prevent the spread of the disease to his other plants.

_____

_____

B5.7 Bacterial diseases

A Fill in the gaps to complete the sentences.

Salmonella is a _____ spread through undercooked food. Symptoms include diarrhoea and vomiting

caused by the _____ produced by the bacteria. In the UK, poultry are _____ against

Salmonella to control the spread of disease.

Gonorrhoea is an STD (_____ transmitted disease). Symptoms include discharge from the

_____ or vagina, and pain on urination. Treatment involves using _____, although many

strains are now resistant. Using a barrier method of contraception (such as _____) and limiting the

number of sexual partners prevents spread.

There are relatively few bacterial diseases of _____ but *Agrobacterium tumefaciens* causes crown galls.

A crown gall is a mass of unspecialised _____ that grows on the shoots.

B Some communicable diseases are caused by bacteria. For each bacterial infection, describe the main symptoms.

a *Salmonella* _____

b Gonorrhoea _____

c *Agrobacterium tumefaciens* infection _____

C *Salmonella* is a type of bacteria that causes food poisoning. It is found in raw meat, usually chicken.

Ella is preparing a chicken salad from the ingredients raw chicken and salad leaves.

Describe three rules she should follow when preparing her salad to make sure she does not cause food poisoning.

1 _____

_____

2 _____

_____

3 _____

_____

D Gonorrhoea is a bacterial disease.

a Describe how it is spread.

_____

b Explain why it is becoming increasingly difficult to treat it with antibiotics.

_____

B5.8 Diseases caused by fungi and protists

A Fill in the gaps to complete the sentences.

Rose black spot is a disease caused by _____. It is spread by wind and water. It damages leaves so they

drop off. This affects growth as _____ is reduced. The spread of the disease is controlled by removing

affected leaves and using chemical sprays.

_____ is caused by protists and is spread by the bite of female mosquitoes. It damages blood and

_____ cells, causes fevers and shaking, and can be fatal. The spread of malaria is reduced by preventing

mosquitoes from breeding, using mosquito _____ to prevent people from being bitten, and using drugs

to kill the parasites in the _____ if a person gets bitten.

B A rose becomes infected with black spot. The diagram below shows one leaf from the plant.

a Estimate the area of the leaf.

Use the formula: area of a circle $= \pi r^2$

HINT When estimating you can use rough figures, for example $\pi = 3$

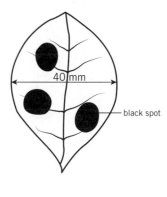

_____

b Estimate the percentage of the leaf that is covered in blackspot.

_____%

C Malaria is a disease that can kill if it is not treated.

The graph shows the annual malaria cases in South Africa between 1971 and 2003.

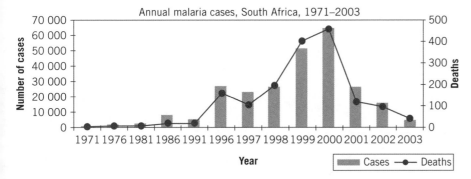

a Describe the pattern in **number of cases** of malaria.

_____

_____

b The mortality rate is the percentage of people who die after contracting a disease.

Calculate the mortality rate of malaria in South Africa in 2001.

Give your answer to 2 decimal places.

_____%

B5.9 Human defence responses

A Fill in the gaps to complete the sentences.

Your body has several lines of defence against the entry of pathogens. The skin is a _____. If you

get cut, _____ in your blood start to form a clot. This dries into a scab, sealing the cut. The skin also

produces antimicrobial secretions that destroy pathogens.

Pathogens can enter the body through the respiratory system. The nose, _____, and bronchi produce

sticky _____ to trap pathogens. Tiny hairs called _____ sweep the mucus up to the back of

the throat where it is swallowed and enters the stomach. The stomach produces strong _____ , which

kills the pathogens in the mucus. It also kills most of the pathogens you take in with _____ and drink.

Your white _____ cells help to defend you against pathogens by ingesting them and by making

_____ and antitoxins.

B The human body has many defence mechanisms.

For each of these parts of the body, describe how they keep pathogens out of the body.

a The skin

_____

_____

b The stomach

_____

_____

C Use the diagram to explain how the cells that line the
respiratory system help defend the body against pathogens.

_____

_____

_____

_____

_____

_____

_____

mucus   goblet cells   cilia

ciliated epithelial cells

D Use the diagrams to describe the three main ways that your white blood cells destroy pathogens.

_____   _____   _____

_____   _____   _____

_____   _____   _____

_____   _____   _____

B5.10 More about plant diseases

A Fill in the gaps to complete the sentences.

Plants can be infected by a range of viral, _____ , and fungal pathogens as well as insect pests.

_____ are insect pests that damage a plant by feeding on sugar-rich sap from the _____

They also act as _____ , transferring pathogens from diseased plants into healthy ones.

Plants can be damaged by a range of ion deficiency conditions. _____ deficiency causes a lack of

growth. Plants need magnesium to make _____ so a magnesium deficiency leads to yellowing of the

leaves known as _____ .

Mineral ions can be replaced by adding _____ to the soil.

B Plants suffer from diseases.

a Explain why diseases caused by mineral deficiency are classed as non-communicable.

_____

b Describe the effect of a magnesium deficiency in plants.

_____

c Explain why this slows down the growth of a plant.

_____

_____

C Aphids are pests that can damage plants and reduce their growth.

a Explain **two** ways that an aphid attack can reduce the growth of a plant.

_____

_____

_____

_____

_____

_____

b Describe **one** way that farmers can destroy aphids.

_____

_____

D A farmer plants wheat in the same field every year. He notices that the growth of the wheat decreases every year. The plants show no other signs of disease.

Suggest a reason for the stunted growth.

Describe what the farmer should do to improve the growth of the wheat.

_____

_____

_____

_____

B5.11 Plant defence responses

A Fill in the gaps to complete the sentences.

Plants have to defend themselves against pathogens, insect pests, and large herbivores.

_____ plant defences against invasion by pathogens include cellulose cell walls, tough waxy

_____ , and layers of bark or dead cells (or dead leaves) which fall off.

Chemical plant defences include _____ chemicals to kill pathogens and poisons to deter herbivores.

Many plants have _____ adaptations against herbivores such as thorns and hairs, leaves that droop or

curl when touched, and _____ to trick animals.

B Plants can become infected by bacteria.

Describe **two** ways that they can defend themselves against bacteria.

1 _____

2 _____

C The passion flower plant has small yellow dots on its leaves that look like butterfly eggs.

a Name this type of defence.

_____

b Explain how it helps protect the plant.

_____

_____

_____

D Describe the similarities and differences between how plants and humans defend themselves against pathogens.

_____

_____

_____

_____

_____

_____

_____

_____

_____

B5 Practice questions

01 Cows can develop painful sores on the bottom of their hooves. These are caused by a bacterial infection.

Scientists carried out research into the effectiveness of antibiotics used to treat the sores.

01.1 Define the term antibiotic. [1 mark]

_____

_____

01.2 The scientists studied 183 different cows from three farms.

The cows were split into four groups and each was given a different treatment. Three groups were treated with different antibiotics and one was treated with a cream that has no antibiotic properties.

The diameter of the sores on the cows' hooves was measured before treatment and then again after 30 days of treatment.

Name the main variables used in this investigation. [2 marks]

Independent variable:

_____

Dependent variable:

_____

01.3 Explain why one group of cows was treated with a cream with no antibiotic properties. [2 marks]

_____

_____

_____

01.4 The results are shown in **Table 1.**

Table 1

Treatment	Mean diameter of sores before treatment in cm	Mean diameter of sores after 30 days of treatment in cm
antibiotic **A**	2.01	1.11
antibiotic **B**	1.95	0.45
antibiotic **C**	2.14	1.29
cream with no antibiotic properties	1.96	2.25

Which antibiotic is the most effective?
Give a reason for your answer. [2 marks]

_____

_____

_____

01.5 Choose the type of graph the scientists should use to display their results.

Give a reason for your answer. [2 marks]

_____

_____

_____

02 Malaria is caused by protists. They are carried inside mosquitoes.

For each of the methods below, explain how they work to control the spread of malaria.

02.1 People take antimalarial drugs. [2 marks]

_____

_____

02.2 Areas of standing water are drained. [2 marks]

_____

_____

03 A student tested how effective three different disinfectants were on stopping the growth of bacteria. They soaked small discs of filter paper in the disinfectants **A**, **B**, **C**, and **D**, and placed them onto a culture plate.

The diagram shows the plate after it had been incubated.

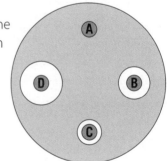

03.1 Describe what the results show. [4 marks]

_____

_____

_____

_____

_____

_____

03.2 The student measured the **diameter** of the clear circle (zone of inhibition) around disc **B**. It was 4.2 cm.

Use the formula: area of a circle $= \pi r^2$

to calculate the area of the clear circle.

Give your answer to 2 significant figures. [2 marks]

_____ cm^2

B5 Checklist

	Student Book	☺	☺	☹
I can define what health is.	5.1			
I can identify the different causes of ill health.	5.1			
I can describe how different types of disease interact.	5.1			
I can define what pathogens are.	5.2			
I can describe how pathogens cause disease.	5.2			
I can describe the ways that pathogens are spread.	5.2			
I can describe how bacteria multiply.	5.3			
I can describe how to grow an uncontaminated culture of bacteria in the lab.	5.3			
I can describe how uncontaminated cultures are used.	5.3			
I can explain why bacteria are cultured at lower temperatures in schools than in industry.	5.3			
I can calculate the number of bacteria in a population.	5.4			
I can describe the effect of disinfectants and antibiotics on bacterial growth.	5.4			
I can describe how the spread of disease can be reduced or prevented.	5.5			
I can give examples of plant and animal diseases caused by viruses.	5.6			
I can give examples of plant and animal diseases caused by bacteria.	5.7			
I can give examples of animal diseases caused by fungi.	5.8			
I can give examples of animal diseases caused by protists.	5.8			
I can describe how the spread of diseases can be reduced or prevented.	5.8			
I can describe how my body stops pathogens getting in.	5.9			
I can explain how my white blood cells protect me from disease.	5.9			
I can describe how mineral deficiencies can cause non-communicable diseases in plants.	5.10			
I can suggest how diseases affect plant growth.	5.10			
I can describe how to detect plant diseases.	5.10			
I can describe some mechanisms that plants use to defend themselves against pathogens and herbivores.	5.11			

B6.1 Vaccination

A Fill in the gaps to complete the sentences.

Pathogens have unique proteins on their surface called _____. A _____ contains small

amounts of dead or inactive forms of a pathogen. When it is injected into your body, your white blood cells produce

_____. These attach to the antigens, destroying the pathogen.

If the same live pathogen re-enters the body, the _____ blood cells respond quickly to produce the

correct antibodies, preventing infection.

If a large proportion of the population is immune to a pathogen, the spread of the pathogen is much reduced.

This is called _____ immunity.

B Label the diagram.

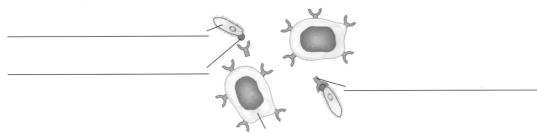

_____

_____

_____

C A tetanus vaccination contains a small amount of inactive tetanus bacteria.

Explain how the vaccination prevents a person getting tetanus.

_____

_____

_____

_____

D Some people have the opinion that vaccination should not be used.

Use data from the graph below as evidence to support vaccination.

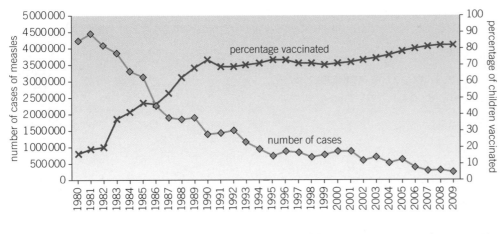

_____

_____

_____

_____

B6.2 Antibiotics and painkillers

A Fill in the gaps to complete the sentences.

_____ such as aspirin treat the symptoms of disease, but do not kill the pathogens that cause it.

_____ cure bacterial diseases by killing the bacterial pathogens inside your body.

Strains of bacteria are evolving that are _____ to antibiotics. This is causing great concern.

Antibiotics do not destroy _____ because they reproduce inside _____. It is difficult to

develop drugs that can destroy them without damaging your tissues.

B A patient has a lung infection. Their doctor prescribes them antibiotics and painkillers.

Explain the function of each drug.

Antibiotic _____

_____

Painkiller _____

_____

C Scientists warn that in the future common infections and minor injuries, which are currently treatable, will become more serious and deadly because bacteria are becoming resistant to many antibiotics.

a Describe one way in which doctors and vets can prevent more types of bacteria becoming resistant to antibiotics.

_____

_____

b Describe one way that scientists can help with the problem.

_____

D Scientists carried out an investigation into how the concentration of antibiotic affected bacteria.

This is the method they followed:

1 Spread bacteria across a culture plate.

2 Add discs soaked in different concentrations of antibiotic (0%, 2.5%, 5%, and 10%) to the plate.

3 Leave the plate in a warm place for 24 hours.

The diagram shows the results. Clear areas around the antibiotic discs, called inhibition zones, show regions where no bacteria have grown.

area where bacteria have grown

sticky tape to seal

| 0% | 2.5% |
| 10% | 5% |

inhibition zones

a Write a conclusion based on the results.

_____

_____

b Describe how the scientists could check the repeatability and reproducibility of their results.

Repeatability _____

Reproducibility _____

B6.3 Discovering drugs

A Fill in the gaps to complete the sentences.

Traditionally drugs were extracted from _____ (e.g., digitalis from foxgloves) or from microorganisms

(e.g., penicillin from _____). Penicillin is an _____ that was discovered by Alexander

_____ . Most new drugs are synthesised by chemists in the pharmaceutical industry. However, the

starting point may still be a chemical extracted from a plant.

B There are a number of drugs used today that are based on traditional medicines extracted from plants and microorganisms.

The bark of the willow tree was used as a painkiller. The active compound it contains is called acetyl salicylic acid, commonly known as aspirin.

Suggest why we now take aspirin for pain relief, rather than willow bark.

_____

_____

_____

_____

C In 1928 Alexander Fleming was growing bacteria on culture plates. He noticed that some spots of mould had started to grow on them. Clear rings were present around the spots of mould.

Write a hypothesis based on this observation.

_____

_____

D Scientists extract a chemical from a plant. They carry out tests to see if it would make a useful antibiotic.

For each test shown below, explain why they carry it out.

a Test to see if it kills bacteria on culture plates.

_____

_____

b Test to see if it destroys human cells.

_____

_____

c Infect live rats with bacteria and test if the chemical cures the infection.

_____

_____

B6.4 Developing drugs

A Fill in the gaps to complete the sentences.

New medical drugs are tested for many _____ before being used in patients. They must be effective,

_____ , stable, and successfully taken into and removed from the body.

New drugs are first tested in the laboratory using cells, tissues, and live _____ . During clinical

_____ the drug is tested on healthy volunteers and patients. Low doses are used to test for

safety. Then larger numbers of patients take to drug to find the best _____ . In double-

_____ trials, some patients are given the drug and others are given a _____ that does not

contain the drug. Neither the patient nor the _____ knows which they are receiving.

B Before they can be prescribed, new drugs are tested for **efficacy, toxicity**, and **dosage.**

Describe why drugs must be tested for:

Efficacy _____

Toxicity _____

Dosage _____

C Scientists are developing a new drug to treat heart disease. There are many stages involved in developing
the drug.

Describe the purpose of each stage shown below:

a The drug is tested on live animals.

_____

b The drug is given to healthy volunteers.

_____

c The drug is given to patients who have heart disease.

_____

D A clinical trial was carried out to test a new flu drug.

220 volunteers were chosen who had the flu. They were split into two groups.

One group were given the drug. The other group was given a placebo.

The volunteers wrote down how they were feeling each day.

a Define 'placebo'.

_____

b Evaluate the method used to test the effectiveness of the drug.

_____

_____

_____

_____

_____

B6.5 Making monoclonal antibodies

A Fill in the gaps to complete the sentences.

Monoclonal antibodies target particular cells or chemicals in the body.

Scientists combine mice _____ (that have been stimulated to make a particular antibody) with

a type of _____ cell to make a cell called a _____ which can divide to make a large

number of identical cells that all produce the same antibodies. These monoclonal antibodies are collected and

_____ .

Monoclonal antibodies are used for home _____ tests or in labs to measure levels of hormones and

other chemicals in the blood and to detect pathogens.

B Describe the function of each of these cells in the production of monoclonal antibodies.

Lymphocytes _____

Tumour _____

Hybridoma _____

C The diagram shows how monoclonal antibodies are made.

Label the structures.

cells taken
from spleen

fusion

mouse injected
with antigen

D When blood forms clots, proteins in the blood form together to form a solid mesh.

Detecting blood clots early means that doctors are able to remove them.

a Explain why it can be harmful to health to develop a blood clot inside the body.

_____

_____

b Explain how using monoclonal antibodies can help doctors detect the location of the blood clots.

_____

_____

_____

B6.6 Uses of monoclonal antibodies

A Fill in the gaps to complete the sentences.

Monoclonal antibodies are used in the treatment of diseases.

They have been developed against the _____ on cancer cells.

If a monoclonal antibody is bound to a radioactive substance, a _____ drug, or a chemical that stops

cells growing and _____, it will deliver the substance to the cancer cells without harming other

_____ in the body.

Monoclonal antibodies have created more _____ effects than expected and are not yet as widely used
as hoped when they were first developed.

B Cancer is caused when the body's own cells start growing and dividing out of control, forming tumours.

a There is risk of damaging healthy cells when treating cancer using traditional methods.

Explain why.

_____

_____

b Monoclonal antibodies can be used to treat cancer.

Label the diagram.

c Describe **one** way that monoclonal antibodies can be used to treat cancer.

_____

_____

d Explain why using monoclonal antibodies to treat cancer reduces the risk of damaging healthy cells.

_____

_____

C Evaluate the reasons why monoclonal antibodies are not widely used to treat cancer.

_____

_____

_____

_____

01 Influenza (the flu) is a communicable disease that can kill very young or elderly people.

01.1 A person who has the flu cannot be treated with antibiotics. Explain why. [2 marks]

_____

_____

_____

01.2 In the UK people over the age of 65 years are offered a free flu vaccination.

Explain how the vaccine prevents a person from getting flu. [4 marks]

_____

_____

_____

_____

_____

_____

_____

01.3 Scientists gathered the data shown in **Figure 1**.

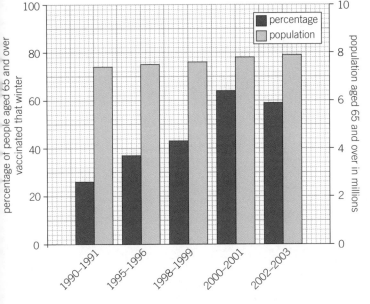

Figure 1

Describe the trend in the percentage of people over 65 having the vaccination between 1990 and 2001. [1 mark]

_____

_____

01.4 Calculate the number of people over 65 who received the flu vaccination in 2000–2001.

Show your working out and give your answer to 1 significant figure. [3 marks]

_____ people

01.5 Explain how a high percentage of people over 65 being vaccinated protects others who have not been vaccinated against flu. [2 marks]

_____

_____

_____

_____

02 New drugs have to be thoroughly tested before they can be given to the public. There are some ethical issues surrounding stages of the drug development process.

Outline the ethical arguments for and against developing new drugs. [4 marks]

_____

_____

_____

_____

_____

_____

_____

_____

_____

_____

_____

B6 Checklist

	Student Book	☺	☻	☹
I can describe how my immune system works.	6.1			
I can explain how vaccination protects me against disease.	6.1			
I can explain what medicines are and how some of them work.	6.2			
I can describe how painkillers and other medicines treat disease symptoms but do not kill pathogens.	6.2			
I can describe the ways in which antibiotics can and cannot be used.	6.2			
I can name some drugs traditionally extracted from plants.	6.3			
I can describe how penicillin was discovered.	6.3			
I can describe how scientists look for new drugs.	6.3			
I can name the stages involved in testing and trialling new drugs.	6.4			
I can explain why testing new drugs is important.	6.4			
I can describe how monoclonal antibodies are produced.	6.5			
I can name some uses of monoclonal antibodies.	6.6			
I can evaluate the use of monoclonal antibodies by evaluating their advantages and disadvantages.	6.6			

B7.1 Non-communicable diseases

A Fill in the gaps to complete the sentences.

Non-communicable diseases cannot be _____ from one individual to another; they are not

infectious. _____ factors are aspects of a person's lifestyle, or substances present in a person's body or

environment, that have been shown to be linked to an _____ rate of a disease. A risk factor for type 2

_____ is overeating.

For some non-communicable diseases, a _____ mechanism for some risk factors has been proven, but

not in others. For example, smoking causes _____ cancer because tar is a carcinogen.

B There are many different risk factors for disease.

a For each risk factor listed below, name one disease that is linked to it.

UV light from the sun _____

Your genes _____

Overeating _____

Smoking cigarettes _____

b From the list above, name one risk factor that:

is an effect of the environment _____

is a lifestyle choice _____

is something that you cannot change _____

C Gethyn has lung cancer. The list below shows some of the impacts of his disease.

P His treatments are making him feel very tired.
Q His treatments are paid for by the NHS.
R His friends and family have spent time looking after him and driving him to hospital appointments.
S He is unable to work.

a Which statement shows a personal impact of the disease? _____

b Which statement shows a social impact? _____

c Which **two** statements have economic impacts? _____ and _____

D 20 children aged 8–16 were selected at random. The length of their feet was measured and they were asked to complete a mental arithmetic test. The scatter graph below shows the data collected.

a Identify a correlation.

_____

_____

_____

b Suggest a possible causal mechanism.

_____

_____

B7.2 Cancer

A Fill in the gaps to complete the sentences.

A tumour forms when there is abnormal, uncontrolled _____ division. _____ tumours

form in one place and do not spread to other tissues. _____ tumour cells are cancers. They invade

neighbouring tissues and may spread to different parts of the body in the blood where they form _____

tumours. They disrupt normal tissues and, if left untreated, may kill the person.

Lifestyle risk factors for cancer include smoking, obesity, viruses, and _____ light. There are also

genetic risk factors for some cancers. Cancer can be treated using _____ during radiotherapy or

_____ , which uses chemicals.

B **a** Label the diagram below to show **normal cells** and **tumour cells**.

b Describe **two** differences between normal cells and tumour cells.

1 _____

_____

2 _____

_____

C Compare the dangers to health of developing benign and malignant tumours.

Include information on how easy it is to treat them.

_____

_____

_____

_____

_____

D Cancer can be treated using radiotherapy.

a Explain how it works.

_____

_____

b Describe a risk associated with radiotherapy.

_____

_____

B7.3 Smoking and risk of disease

A Fill in the gaps to complete the sentences.

Tobacco smoke contains many substances including the addictive drug _____, the poisonous gas

carbon _____ , and the carcinogen _____ .

Smoking can cause cardiovascular disease including coronary _____ disease, _____ cancer,

and lung diseases such as _____ and COPD. If a pregnant woman smokes, her blood carries carbon

monoxide, which restricts the amount of _____ the fetus gets. This can lead to premature birth, low

_____ , and even stillbirth.

B Tobacco smoke contains the harmful substances **nicotine**, **carbon monoxide**, and **tar**.

For each of the health problems below, suggest which substance in tobacco smoke causes it.

a Breakdown of alveoli _____

b Increase in blood pressure _____

c A low birth weight of babies born to women who smoke whilst pregnant _____

d Throat cancer _____

C Carlos studies the graph opposite.

He draws a conclusion based on the data: If you smoke then you will get lung cancer.

Correct his conclusion.

_____

_____

_____

_____

_____

_____

_____

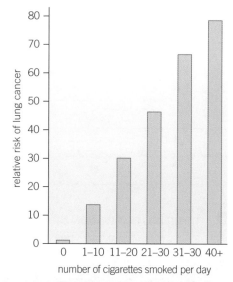

D Smoking is linked to cardiovascular disease (CVD).

Study the table opposite.

Calculate:

a The increase in number of deaths in men between those who do not smoke and those who smoke 12 cigarettes a day.

Cigarettes smoked per day	CVD deaths per 100 000 men per year
0	572
10 (range 1–14)	802
20 (range 15–24)	892
30 (range >24)	1025

_____ per 100 000 men per year

b The percentage of men who died from CVD that smoked more than 24 cigarettes a day.

Give your answer to one significant figure.

_____%

B7.4 Diet, exercise, and disease

A Fill in the gaps to complete the sentences.

Eating more food than you need could make you _____ . This can lead to serious health problems such

as type 2 _____ , high _____ pressure, and heart disease.

Regular _____ lowers blood cholesterol and reduces the risk of _____ deposits building up

in the coronary arteries, lowering the risk of _____ disease.

B The food you eat transfers energy, which your body uses for the basic reactions that keep you alive. The rate the
energy is transferred is called your metabolic rate. As you age, this decreases.

Some energy is also used to digest your food and for physical activity.

Use this information, and your knowledge, to suggest why many people gain weight as they get older.

_____

_____

_____

_____

_____

C Explain the causal mechanisms that explain why people who exercise regularly are healthier than people who don't.

_____

_____

_____

_____

_____

D The graphs below show the effect of obesity on the risk of developing type 2 diabetes.

Describe **two** observations from the graphs.

1 _____

_____

2 _____

_____

B7.5 Alcohol and other carcinogens

A Fill in the gaps to complete the sentences.

Alcohol is an addictive drug that affects the _____ system. A small amount makes people feel relaxed

and _____ down their reactions. Drinking a large dose can lead to unconsciousness, _____ ,

and even death. Long-term use can cause cirrhosis, _____ cancer, and brain damage. Alcohol taken in

by a _____ woman can affect the development of her unborn baby.

Ionising radiation is a risk factor for cancer because it causes _____ in the DNA. An example is ultraviolet

(UV) light from the _____ , which increases the risk of _____ cancers.

B Long-term use of alcohol can lead to death.

a Name the main **two** organs that are damaged by drinking alcohol.

1 _____

2 _____

b The graph shows the number of alcohol-related deaths in men in the UK.

Describe the trend shown.

_____

_____

_____

_____

_____

_____

C The following information is from a website belonging to a company who fit equipment to remove radon gas from homes.

> Radon is a radioactive gas, which can cause cancer. Levels are particularly high in granite-rich areas.
> An active radon sump, fitted with a fan, is the best way to reduce indoor radon levels in your home.
> The cost to fit the system is £1000.
> The continuous running cost of the fan will normally be around £2 per week.

Jay is considering fitting an active radon sump in his house.

a Explain why radon gas is a risk factor for lung cancer.

_____

_____

b Estimate the **total** cost of the system in the first year.

_____

_____

c The company claim that 'An active radon sump, fitted with a fan, is the best way to reduce indoor radon levels in your home.'

Suggest what is needed before this claim can be believed.

_____

_____

_____

_____

B7 Practice questions

01 Mouth cancer is where a tumour develops on the surface of the tongue, mouth, lips, or gums.

It is a non-communicable disease.

Define the following terms.

01.1 Tumour [1 mark]

_____

_____

01.2 Non-communicable disease [1 mark]

_____

_____

02 **Figure 1** shows the effects of smoking and drinking alcohol on the risk of developing mouth cancer.

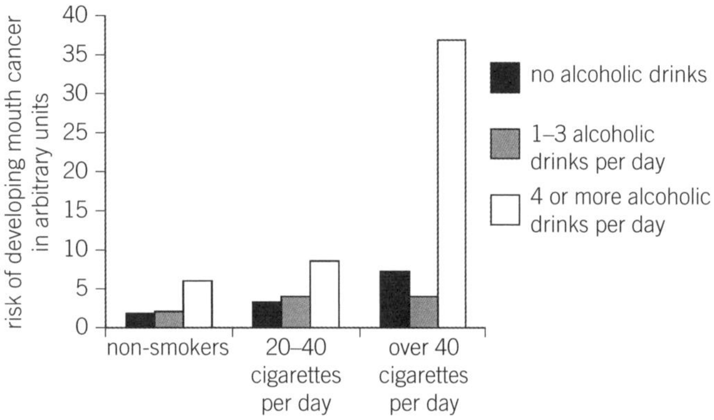

Figure 1

02.1 Draw conclusions from the data. [3 marks]

_____

_____

_____

_____

_____

02.2 A doctor carries out a survey on some of her patients.

During an interview she asks five patients, on average, how many cigarettes they smoke per day and how much alcohol they drink.

The information is shown in **Table 1**.

Table 1

Patient	Average number of cigarettes smoked per day	Average number of alcoholic drinks per day
A	22	2
B	0	5
C	45	4
D	0	1
E	30	6

Add letters to the boxes below to order the patients' risk for developing mouth cancer.

Use the data on the graph. [2 marks]

Low risk → High risk

☐ ☐ ☐ ☐ ☐

02.3 Give **one** reason why this information may not be accurate [1 mark]

_____

_____

03 A group of scientists decide to carry out research using rats.

This is their method:

- Use 5 groups of 10 rats.
- Give each group a different volume of alcohol per day for 6 months.
- Use a microscope to study the mouth tissues of each rat to identify and count any tumour cells.

03.1 Give a prediction for their investigation, based on the data in **Figure 1**. [1 mark]

_____

_____

03.2 Evaluate the advantages and disadvantages of using rats, rather than humans, in this research. [4 marks]

_____

_____

_____

_____

_____

_____

_____

_____

_____

_____

_____

_____

_____

_____

_____

_____

B7 Checklist

	Student Book	☺	☺	☹
I can define non-communicable disease.	7.1			
I can define lifestyle factor.	7.1			
I can describe how scientists consider risk.	7.1			
I can describe the human and financial costs involved in non-communicable diseases.	7.1			
I can define causal mechanism.	7.1			
I can describe what a tumour is.	7.2			
I can explain the difference between benign and malignant tumours.	7.2			
I can describe how cancer spreads.	7.2			
I can explain how smoking affects the risk of developing cardiovascular disease.	7.3			
I can explain how smoking affects the risk of developing lung disease and lung cancer.	7.3			
I can describe the effect of smoking on unborn babies.	7.3			
I can describe the effect of diet and exercise on the development of obesity.	7.4			
I can describe how diet and exercise affect the risk of developing cardiovascular disease.	7.4			
I can describe obesity as a risk factor for type 2 diabetes.	7.4			
I can describe alcohol as a factor that affects liver and brain function.	7.5			
I can describe alcohol as a factor that can affect unborn babies.	7.5			
I can describe alcohol as a carcinogen.	7.5			
I can name other agents that act as carcinogens.	7.5			

B8.1 Photosynthesis

A Fill in the gaps to complete the sentences.

Photosynthesis is an _____ reaction that takes place in the cells in _____ and

plant leaves. Energy is transferred from the environment to the chloroplast by _____ . It is used to

convert carbon dioxide and _____ into sugar (glucose).

A green substance called _____ captures the light.

Photosynthesis can be summarised as follows: carbon dioxide + water → _____ + oxygen.

Leaves are well adapted to allow the maximum amount of photosynthesis to take place.

B Complete the word and symbol equations for **photosynthesis**.

_____

carbon dioxide + _____ ⟶ glucose + _____

6 _____   6H$_2$0   ⟶ _____ + 6O$_2$

C A student carried out an experiment using the equipment shown below.

bubbles

pondweed

Describe how they could prove that the bubbles contained oxygen.

_____

_____

D The leaves of a plant are adapted to carry out photosynthesis.

For each adaptation below, explain how it increases the efficiency of photosynthesis.

a Broad shape

_____

_____

b Veins running through the leaf

_____

_____

c Leaves are very thin

_____

_____

B8.2 The rate of photosynthesis

A Fill in the gaps to complete the sentences.

The rate of photosynthesis may be affected by _____ intensity, temperature, concentration of

_____ _____ , and chlorophyll levels in the leaf. These are known as _____

factors because at times any one or several of these things can be in short supply and limit the rate.

For most plants the _____ the light, the faster the rate of photosynthesis. As temperature rises, the rate

of photosynthesis _____ up to a certain temperature. After this, _____ are denatured and

the rate falls. Increasing the concentration of carbon dioxide will _____ the rate of photosynthesis.

B A group of students were asked to investigate the effect of light intensity on the rate of photosynthesis.

They decided to shine a lamp on some pondweed in a test tube of water. They are going to change the distance of the lamp to the pondweed.

a Name the independent variable. _____

b Suggest a suitable dependent variable.

c Give **two** control variables that they should use.

1 _____

2 _____

C The students used a distance of 10 cm, 20 cm, 30 cm, and 40 cm.

Explain what happened to the light intensity as the distance increased by 10 cm. Use the **inverse square law**.

_____

_____

D On the axes below, draw a line to show the expected results from this investigation.

rate of photosynthesis (y-axis), light intensity (x-axis)

E In certain conditions, the amount of photosynthesis a plant can carry out is limited. This is due to **limiting factors**. Light intensity is an example of a limiting factor.

Write **three** other limiting factors for photosynthesis.

1 _____

2 _____

3 _____

B8.3 How plants use glucose

A Fill in the gaps to complete the sentences.

Plant and algal cells use the glucose produced during photosynthesis for _____ to transfer energy. They

also convert the glucose into insoluble _____ for storage, and use it to produce fats or oils for storage,

_____ to strengthen cell walls, and amino acids.

Plants and algal cells also need _____ ions absorbed from the soil or water to make amino acids.

The amino acids are joined together to make _____ .

B You can test a leaf for the presence of **starch**.

Describe the purpose of each stage in the method:

a Leave the leaf in boiling water for 5 minutes.

_____

b Turn off the Bunsen burner.

_____

c Place a test tube of ethanol into the hot water. Add the leaf to the ethanol.

_____

C The diagram shows three leaves, A, B, and C on a plant.

Before starch test

A   B   C

green leaf   black paper   green areas   white areas

Results

Explanation for results

The plant was left in the light for 2 days.

The leaves were removed and were tested for starch.

Use a blue or black pen to colour in the leaves to show the results of the test.

In the box underneath each leaf, give a reason for the result.

D Plants produce glucose during photosynthesis. Give **four** ways that plants use glucose.

1 _____

2 _____

3 _____

4 _____

B8.4 Making the most of photosynthesis

A Fill in the gaps to complete the sentences.

Commercial greenhouses control the temperature and the levels of light and _____ _____

to get the fastest possible rates of _____. As a result, the plants _____ as quickly as possible.

The plants can be grown in water with a perfect balance of nutrients. This is known as _____.

Growers have to choose the _____ conditions for growth, whilst still making a profit.

B Explain how each labelled part of the greenhouse in the diagram increases the rate of photosynthesis.

You should use **limiting factors** in your answers.

Ventilation vents

_____

_____

_____

_____

Paraffin heater

_____

_____

Automatic watering system

_____

_____

Automatic lights

_____

_____

ventilation vents

electric lighting

automatic watering system

paraffin heater

C The graph shows how changing the conditions in a greenhouse affect the rate of photosynthesis.

a Name the conditions needed for a maximum rate of photosynthesis.

_____

_____

b A grower decides to use a temperature of 20 °C.

Suggest why.

_____

_____

rate of photosynthesis

high CO$_2$ 30 °C

high CO$_2$ 20 °C

low CO$_2$ 20 °C

light intensity

B8 Practice questions

01 A student carried out an investigation into how a limiting factor affects the rate of photosynthesis.

The equipment they used is shown in **Figure 1**.

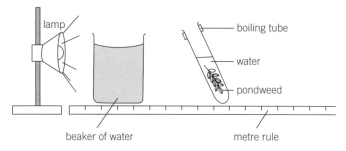

Figure 1

This is the method they used:

1 Place the pondweed 30 cm (0.30 m) away from the lamp.

2 Count the number of bubbles produced in 1 minute.

3 Repeat, moving the lamp closer to the pondweed by 5 cm (0.05 m) each time.

01.1 Which limiting factor is the student investigating?

[1 mark]

_____

01.2 Explain the purpose of the beaker of water.

[2 marks]

_____
_____
_____

01.3 Their results are shown in **Table 1**.

Table 1

Distance of lamp from pondweed in m	Number of gas bubbles produced in 1 minute
0.30	3
0.25	8
0.20	15
0.15	25
0.10	27
0.05	27

Use the inverse square law to calculate a value for the light intensity when the lamp was 0.10 m away from the pondweed. [2 marks]

_____

01.4 Describe the pattern in the results. [2 marks]

_____
_____
_____
_____
_____

01.5 Give an explanation for this pattern. [4 marks]

_____
_____
_____
_____
_____
_____
_____
_____
_____
_____
_____
_____
_____

01.6 Describe **two** reasons why the results may not be accurate.

Explain changes in the method that would improve the accuracy of the results. [5 marks]

_____
_____
_____
_____
_____
_____
_____
_____
_____
_____
_____
_____
_____

B8 Checklist

	Student Book	☺	☺	☹
I can identify the raw materials and energy source for photosynthesis.	8.1			
I can describe photosynthesis as an endothermic reaction.	8.1			
I can write the equations that summarise photosynthesis.	8.1			
I can explain how humans can manipulate the environment in which plants grow.	8.1			
I can name the factors that limit the rate of photosynthesis in plants.	8.2			
I can describe how plants use the glucose they make.	8.3			
I can name the extra materials that plant cells need to produce proteins.	8.3			
I can describe some practical tests for starch, sugars, and proteins.	8.3			
I can describe how the different factors affecting the rate of photosynthesis interact.	8.4			

B9.1 Aerobic respiration

A Fill in the gaps to complete the sentences.

Aerobic respiration is an _____ reaction that takes place in all living cells. It can be summarised as:

glucose + _____ → _____ _____ + water (+ energy transferred to

the environment)

Most stages take place in the _____ of the cells. The _____ transferred is needed for living

processes. Some organisms, such as humans, need it for keeping warm.

B a Write the word and balanced symbol equation for **aerobic respiration**.

Word equation

_____ + _____ → _____ + _____ _____

Balanced symbol equation

_____ + _____ → _____ + _____

b During respiration, energy is transferred but it is not included in the equation.
Explain why.

_____

_____

C Harriet starts bodybuilding. The percentage of her body that is muscle increases from 26% to 32%.

The amount of food that her body needs to function at rest also increases. Explain why.

_____

_____

_____

_____

_____

D The energy transferred during respiration supplies all the energy needed for living processes in the cells.

Describe why the following cells need energy.

a a sperm cell

_____

_____

b a plant root hair cell

_____

_____

B9.2 The response to exercise

A Fill in the gaps to complete the sentences.

When you exercise your _____ help you move around. They need energy to contract.

During exercise the human body responds to the increased demand for energy. Body responses to exercise include:

- increases in the _____ rate, the breathing rate, and the breath volume
- _____ stores in the muscles are converted to glucose for respiration
- the flow of oxygenated _____ to the muscles increases.

These responses act to increase the rate of supply of glucose and _____ to the muscles.

They also increase the rate of removal of _____ _____ from the muscles.

B When you exercise changes take place in your body. One example is that your heart rate will increase.

a Describe what happens to:

Your breathing _____

The glycogen stored in your muscles _____

b Explain why your heart rate increases.

_____

_____

_____

C Chloe was asked what happens to the **rate of respiration** during exercise.

This was her answer: 'The rate of respiration increases, which brings more oxygen to the cells.'

Correct her answer.

_____

_____

_____

D Four Year 10 students measured their pulse rates at rest. They then ran on a treadmill at a speed of 8 km/h for 5 minutes and measured their pulse rates during the run.

The results are shown in the table.

Student	Pulse rate in beats per min	
	At rest	Maximum during exercise
Jasmine	80	162
Louise	72	149
Brandon	84	159
Ruby	65	139

Draw **three** conclusions from the results:

1 _____

_____

2 _____

_____

3 _____

_____

B9.3 Anaerobic respiration

A Fill in the gaps to complete the sentences.

Anaerobic respiration is respiration without _____ .

When you exercise hard, your blood might not be able to supply the muscles with enough _____ so

they use anaerobic respiration. The lactic acid produced makes muscles tired. After exercise, oxygen is still needed to

break down the acid that has built up. The amount of oxygen needed is known as the oxygen _____ .

Anaerobic respiration in cells and some microorganisms, such as yeast, results in the production of

_____ and carbon dioxide.

B Complete the word equations for anaerobic respiration in different organisms:

Animals: glucose → _____ _____

Plants and some microorganisms: glucose → _____ + _____ _____

C Compare aerobic and anaerobic respiration in animal cells.

_____

_____

_____

_____

D The breathing rate of two people of different fitness levels was taken before, during, and after intense exercise.
The graph shows the results.

a The recovery time is how long it takes for breathing rate to go back to the resting rate after exercise.

Estimate the recovery time for each person:

Unfit _____

Fit _____

b Explain why breathing rate remains high after exercise.

_____

_____

c Explain the difference in recovery rates between the two people.

_____

_____

B9.4 Metabolism and the liver

A Fill in the gaps to complete the sentences.

The energy transferred by _____ in cells is used by the organism for the enzyme-controlled metabolic

processes that synthesise new molecules or break molecules down.

These include:

● The conversion of _____ to starch, glycogen, and cellulose

● The formation of lipid molecules

● The use of glucose and nitrate ions to form _____ acids, which are used to synthesise proteins

● The breakdown of excess proteins to form _____ , which takes place in the _____ .

One important role of the liver is to remove lactic acid produced by _____ respiration. Blood flowing

through the muscles transports lactic acid to the liver where it is converted back to _____ .

B Define 'metabolism'.

_____

_____

C Name each of the metabolic processes being described.

a Reaction where energy is transferred from glucose molecules _____

b Process carried out by green plants and algae to produce food molecules _____

D During anaerobic respiration in the muscles lactic acid is produced.

Describe how lactic acid is removed from the body.

_____

_____

_____

_____

B9 Practice questions

01 Yeast is a single celled fungus. It carries out anaerobic respiration.

01.1 Complete the word equation for this reaction.

[1 mark]

glucose → _____ + carbon dioxide

01.2 A student was asked to carry out an investigation into how temperature affects the rate of anaerobic respiration in yeast.

Her prediction is: 'the higher the temperature, the faster the rate of respiration'.

Figure 1 shows how the student set up her equipment.

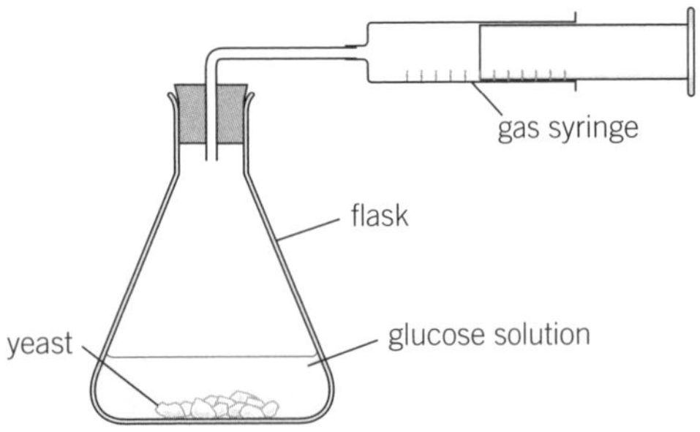

Figure 1

Give the function of the gas syringe. [1 mark]

_____

01.3 The student has made one mistake in setting up the equipment.

Describe what this is and why it needs to be corrected. [2 marks]

_____

_____

_____

01.4 The student corrects the mistake.

Explain how she could use the equipment in **Figure 1** to carry out her investigation. [4 marks]

HINT She will need to use other equipment as well. Make sure you mention the variables she should use.

_____

_____

_____

_____

_____

_____

_____

_____

01.5 The student plotted her results as a line graph as shown in **Figure 2**.

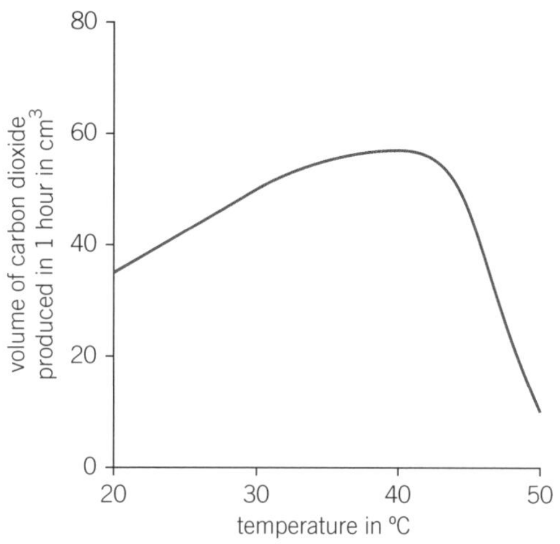

Figure 2

Describe what the graph shows about how temperature affects the rate of anaerobic respiration in yeast.

Write down whether it supports the student's prediction or not. Give a reason for your answer.

[4 marks]

_____

_____

_____

_____

_____

_____

_____

_____

01.6 Give a scientific explanation for what happens to the rate at temperatures over 40 °C. [3 marks]

_____

_____

_____

_____

_____

B9 Checklist

	Student Book	☺	☺	☹
I can write the equations that summarise aerobic respiration.	9.1			
I can explain why cellular respiration is important.	9.1			
I can describe how my body responds to the increased demands for energy during exercise.	9.2			
I can explain why less energy is transferred by anaerobic respiration than by aerobic respiration.	9.3			
I can explain what is meant by oxygen debt.	9.3			
I can describe how anaerobic respiration can take place in lots of different organisms, including plants, bacteria, and fungi.	9.3			
I can define metabolism.	9.4			
I can describe how the liver is involved in repaying the oxygen debt.	9.4			

B10.1 Principles of homeostasis

A Fill in the gaps to complete the sentences.

Homeostasis is the control of the _____ conditions of a cell or organism.

It is important for maintaining suitable conditions for cell functions, including enzyme action.

In the human body homeostasis includes control of blood _____ concentration, body temperature, and

water levels. The control systems are automatic and may involve _____ or chemical responses.

All control systems include _____ , coordination centres, and effectors.

B Give **three** internal conditions controlled by homeostasis in humans.

1 _____

2 _____

3 _____

C Devin is exercising on a hot day. He does not stop to drink any water or eat any food.

Explain what happens to the internal conditions you named in activity **B**.

1 _____

_____

2 _____

_____

3 _____

_____

D Name the key features of a control system.

a Cells that detect stimuli _____

b Receive and process information _____

c Muscles or glands that bring about a response _____

B10.2 The structure and function of the human nervous system

A Fill in the gaps to complete the sentences.

The nervous system uses _____ impulses to enable you to react quickly to your surroundings and

coordinate your behaviour. Cells called receptors detect _____ (changes in the environment).

Impulses from receptors pass along _____ neurones to the central nervous system (CNS), which is

made up of the brain and _____ cord. The brain coordinates the response, and impulses are sent along

_____ neurones from the brain to the effector organs.

Effector organs may be _____ or glands.

B Label the sense organs and the type of receptors they contain on the diagram. Some will have more than one type of receptor.

sense organ

receptors it contains

C Jules catches a ball that is thrown towards her. Finish the explanation of what happens. Include the words below.

sensory neurones   **CNS**   **motor neurones**   **muscles**   **electrical impulses**   **effectors**

The light receptors in her eyes detect the movement of the ball....

_____

_____

_____

_____

_____

_____

_____

neurone **A**   neurone **B**

D The diagram shows two neurones, **A** and **B**.

neurone endings in an effector

a Name the neurones:

A _____

receptor

B _____

b Draw an arrow under each neurone to show the direction of impulses.

B10.3 Reflex actions

A Fill in the gaps to complete the sentences.

Reflex actions are _____ and rapid and do not involve the conscious parts of the _____ .

They control everyday bodily functions, such as breathing and digestion, and help you to avoid _____ .

The main stages of a reflex arc are:

stimulus → receptor → sensory neurone → _____ neurone → motor neurone →

_____ → response

At junctions between neurones are tiny gaps called _____ . Impulses travel across them using

_____ that diffuse across the gap.

B Pulling your hand away from a hot object is an example of a reflex action.

a Reflex actions are automatic. Explain what this means.

_____

b The impulses travel along the neurones involved in a reflex action at a speed of 120 m/s.

Calculate how long it would take an impulse to travel 3 m.

_____ s

c Explain why it is important that they are fast.

_____

_____

C The diagram opposite shows the pathway of a reflex action (a reflex arc).

Write the letter (**U–Z**) that shows:

a sensory neurone ☐   a receptor ☐

a motor neurone ☐   an effector ☐

a relay neurone ☐   a synapse ☐

white matter
grey matter↓
U
Z
V
W
X
Y

neurone C

D Neurones in the nervous system are separated by tiny gaps. The diagram opposite shows this.

impulse arrives in neurone

A

neurone D

a Name the gap, labelled **A** on the diagram. _____

b Electrical impulses cannot cross the gap.

Use the diagram to describe how a new electrical impulse is started up in neurone **D**.

_____

_____

_____

_____

B10.4 The brain

A Fill in the gaps to complete the sentences.

The brain is made up of billions of interconnected _____ that control complex behaviour.

The cerebral cortex, the cerebellum, and the _____ are regions of the brain.

It also contains the _____, which is involved in controlling body temperature and the pituitary gland,

which produces _____.

Scientists map regions of the brain to their functions by studying patients with brain damage, by electrically

stimulating different areas of the brain, and by using _____ scanning techniques.

B The diagram shows regions of the brain labelled X, Y, and Z.
Complete the table by:

● writing a letter in the middle column.
● describing the function of each region.

Region of the brain	Letter	Function
medulla		
cerebral cortex		
cerebellum		

C Describe why it is difficult to:

a study the brain.

_____

_____

b treat brain disorders.

_____

_____

_____

D Functional magnetic resonance imaging (fMRI) measures changes that occur within the brain.

Suggest why it is a useful tool for diagnosing brain disorders.

_____

_____

_____

_____

B10.5 The eye

A Fill in the gaps to complete the sentences.

The eye is a sense organ containing receptors in the _____ that are sensitive to light.

The tough outer _____ has a transparent region at the front called the _____ that lets light

in and _____ (changes the direction of) light towards the retina.

The iris controls the size of the _____ and the amount of light entering the eye.

The ciliary muscles and suspensory ligaments change the shape of the _____ to focus light on to the retina.

The _____ nerve carries impulses from the retina to the _____ .

B The diagram below shows a cross-section of a human eye.

A ....

E ....

D ....

B ....

lens

C ....

Write which parts are labelled by **A**, **B**, **C**, **D**, and **E**.

A _____   D _____

B _____   E _____

C _____

C The diagram shows how the pupil responds to bright light.

This is an example of a reflex action.

brain is part of CNS

_____ neurone

bright light is detected
by cells on the retina at
the back of the eye

muscles in iris contract

pupil is smaller

_____ neurone

a Name the nerve that contains neurones to and from the eye to the brain.

_____

b Write the correct name of the neurones on the diagram.

c Use the diagram to explain how the pupil changes shape when a bright light shines in it.

_____

_____

_____

d Suggest a reason for this reflex action.

_____

D Explain how light from an object forms an image on the retina.

_____

_____

_____

A Fill in the gaps to complete the sentences.

Accommodation is the process of changing the shape of the _____ of the eye to focus on near or distant objects.

To focus on close objects the ciliary muscles _____, the suspensory ligaments loosen, and the lens becomes _____ so it can refract light rays strongly.

To focus on _____ objects the _____ muscles relax, the suspensory ligaments are pulled _____, and the lens is pulled thinner so it only refracts the light rays slightly.

Sight defects can be treated using spectacle lenses and _____ lenses, which refract light rays so they focus on the retina. They can also be treated by laser surgery or replacement lenses in the eye.

B Define the science term **accommodation**.

_____

C Describe how the eye focuses on a distant object. Mention the changes that take place to the cillary muscles, suspensory ligaments, and lens. Use the diagram below to help you.

_____

_____

_____

D Diagram **A** shows the eye of a person with an eye defect.

Diagram **B** shows one way of correcting the defect.

a Name the defect shown in diagram **A**.

_____

_____

A

B

concave lens

b Explain why the person cannot see objects clearly.

_____

_____

c Complete the ray diagram on diagram **B** to show how the correction works.

B10 Practice questions

01 A group of six students investigated reaction times. This is the method they followed:

1 Stand in a circle holding hands.

2 A separate person acts as the timer. They start a stop-clock and shout 'start'.

3 Person 1 squeezes the hand of person 2. When person 2 feels the squeeze, they squeeze the hand of person 3 and so the 'squeeze' is passed around the circle back to person 1.

4 When person 1 feels the squeeze they shout 'stop' and the timer stops the stop-clock.

5 Repeat three more times.

Their results are shown in **Table 1**.

Table 1

Trial	Time taken for 'squeeze' to travel around the circle in s
1	5.8
2	5.0
3	4.8
4	4.7

01.1 One of the results is anomalous.

Identify which one, and give a possible reason why. [2 marks]

_____

_____

_____

01.2 Calculate the mean time taken for the 'squeeze' to travel around the circle. [2 marks]

_____ s

01.3 Use the mean to calculate an average reaction time for each person in the circle. [2 marks]

_____ s

01.4 Describe what the students should do in order to increase the repeatability of their results [2 marks]

_____

_____

01.5 The students decide that this method is not an accurate way of measuring each person's reaction time.

Suggest a more suitable method. [1 mark]

_____

_____

02 A common defect of the eye is hyperopia (long-sightedness).

02.1 Compare the vision of a person with hyperopia with the vision of someone with normal vision. [2 marks]

_____

_____

02.2 Suggest **one** way that the eye of a person with hyperopia is different from that of someone with normal vision. [1 mark]

_____

02.3 One way to correct hyperopia is to use contact lenses. Another method is to wear spectacles.

Give **one** advantage and **one** disadvantage of using contact lenses rather than spectacles to correct vision. [2 marks]

Advantage _____

_____

_____

_____

Disadvantage _____

_____

_____

_____

B10 Checklist

	Student Book	☺	😐	☹
I can explain why it is important to control the internal environment.	10.1			
I can name the key elements of control systems.	10.1			
I can explain why we need a nervous system.	10.2			
I can explain how the structure of the nervous system is adapted to its function.	10.2			
I can explain how receptors enable us to respond to changes in our surroundings.	10.2			
I can explain what reflexes are.	10.3			
I can describe how reflexes work.	10.3			
I can explain why reflexes are important in the body.	10.3			
I can describe what the main areas of the brain do.	10.4			
I can describe how scientists find out about the structure and functions of the brain.	10.4			
I can name the main parts of the human eye and describe how the structures are related to their functions.	10.5			
I can describe how the eye focuses light.	10.5			
I can describe how the eye focuses on near and distant objects.	10.6			
I can describe what happens in short-sightedness and long-sightedness and how these problems can be solved.	10.6			

B11.1 Principles of hormonal control

A Fill in the gaps to complete the sentences.

The _____ system is made up of glands that secrete chemicals called _____ directly into

the bloodstream. The blood carries the hormone to a _____ organ where it produces an effect.

Compared with the _____ system, the effects of hormones are often slower but longer lasting.

The pituitary gland is the _____ gland and secretes several hormones, some of which act on

other glands.

B The diagram below shows the main endocrine glands of the human body.

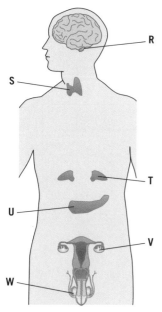

Complete the table to name the glands and the hormone it secretes.

Letter	Name of gland	Hormone it secretes
R		FSH (in women)
S		thyroxine
T	adrenal gland	
U		insulin
V		oestrogen
W	testis (male)	

C Give **two** differences between typical nervous and hormonal responses.

1 _____

2 _____

D Explain why the pituitary gland is known as the master gland.

_____

_____

B11.2 The control of blood glucose levels

A Fill in the gaps to complete the sentences.

Your blood glucose levels are monitored and controlled by your _____. This organ produces the

hormone _____, which allows glucose to move from the blood into the cells and to be stored as

_____ in the liver and muscles. It also produces _____, which allows glycogen to be

converted back into glucose and released into the _____. These two hormones interact with each other

in a _____ feedback cycle to control glucose levels.

In type _____ diabetes, the blood glucose may rise to fatally high levels because the pancreas does not

secrete enough (or any) insulin. In type _____ diabetes, the body stops responding to its own insulin.

B Describe what the following three substances are:

Glycogen _____

Glucose _____

Glucagon _____

C Complete the flow diagram to show the steps in the negative feedback cycle involved in controlling blood
glucose levels.

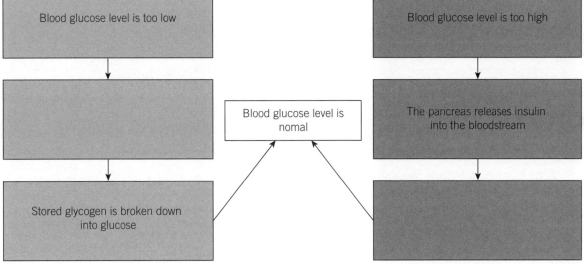

D Explain why:

a People with type 1 diabetes have to inject themselves with insulin.

_____

_____

b Eating too much food can lead to obesity

_____

_____

B11.3 Treating diabetes

A Fill in the gaps to complete the sentences.

Type 1 diabetes is normally controlled by injecting _____ to replace the hormone that is not made in

the body.

Type 2 diabetes is often treated by controlling the amount of _____ in the diet and taking more

_____ . If this doesn't work, _____ may be needed.

B Two people were given a drink high in glucose and their blood glucose levels were monitored.

The graph opposite shows the results.

a Which person, **X** or **Y**, has diabetes? _____

b Explain how you made your decision.

_____

_____

_____

_____

C Type 1 diabetes cannot be cured, but it can be treated.

Explain what this means.

_____

_____

_____

_____

D Cerys is nine. She was diagnosed with type 1 diabetes two years ago.

Her mother is pregnant with her baby sister. Her parents decide to take stem cells from the baby's umbilical cord once she is born. These cells will be frozen so they can be stored.

Explain why they decide to do this.

_____

_____

_____

_____

_____

_____

_____

B11.4 The role of negative feedback

A Fill in the gaps to complete the sentences.

_____ from the thyroid gland stimulates the basal _____ rate. It plays an important role in

growth and development.

Adrenaline is produced by the _____ glands in times of fear or stress. It increases the heart rate and

boosts the delivery of _____ and glucose to the brain and muscles, preparing the body for 'fight or

_____.'

Thyroxine is controlled by _____ feedback whereas adrenaline is not.

B Thyroxine is a hormone secreted by the thyroid gland. Its release is controlled by another hormone, called
thyroid-stimulating hormone, or TSH.

Use the diagram to help you answer the following questions.

a Name the gland that releases TSH.

_____

b Explain how negative feedback helps keep the levels of thyroxine in the body relatively constant.

_____

_____

_____

_____

C Oscar is at a birthday party. Suddenly, one of the party balloons next to him bursts and makes a loud noise.

Describe how this affects Oscar's body.

You should include the effects of adrenaline, and explain why this hormone is released.

_____

_____

_____

_____

_____

_____

B11.5 Human reproduction

A Fill in the gaps to complete the sentences.

During _____ reproductive hormones cause secondary _____ characteristics to develop.

Oestrogen is the main female reproductive hormone produced by the _____ . At puberty eggs begin to

mature and one is released approximately every 28 days during a process called _____ .

Hormones involved in the _____ cycle of a woman include _____ stimulating hormone

(FSH), luteinising hormone (LH), oestrogen, and _____ .

_____ is the main male reproductive hormone produced by the _____ . It stimulates

sperm production.

B Label the diagram of the female reproductive system.

C Use the descriptions to name each of the parts of the male reproductive system:

a Carries sperm from where it is produced to the urethra _____

b Keeps the testes away from the body for maximum sperm production _____

c Makes sperm _____

d Places sperm into the vagina _____

D The roles of two different female reproductive hormones, **X** and **Y**, are shown in the table below.

Hormone X	Hormone Y
Stimulates the build-up of the uterus lining	Maintains the uterus lining
Triggers the development of female secondary sexual characteristics	A decrease triggers menstruation

a Name each hormone:

X _____

Y _____

b Name the gland that secretes both of these hormones.

_____

c Describe how these hormones travel from this gland to the uterus.

_____

d Give **two** female secondary sexual characteristics.

1 _____

2 _____

B11.6 Hormones and the menstrual cycle

A Fill in the gaps to complete the sentences.

FSH from the _____ gland stimulates eggs to mature in the follicles of the ovary and the ovary to

produce _____.

_____ secreted by the ovaries stimulates the growth of the lining of the _____ and the

release of LH and inhibits _____.

LH stimulates _____.

_____ is produced by the empty follicle after ovulation. It maintains the lining of the uterus and inhibits

FSH and LH.

B The diagram opposite shows the main events of the menstrual cycle.

Write down the days in the 28-day cycle on which these events take place:

a Ovulation _____

b The uterus lining builds up

_____

c The uterus lining is maintained

_____

C Use the diagram in activity **B** to explain how FSH, LH, oestrogen, and progesterone interact in order to control the events in the menstrual cycle.

_____

_____

_____

_____

_____

_____

_____

D If a woman becomes pregnant, the placenta will produce progesterone.

Explain why this is important for the development of the embryo.

_____

_____

_____

B11.7 The artificial control of fertility

A Fill in the gaps to complete the sentences.

To prevent pregnancy you need to prevent the egg and _____ meeting, or prevent a fertilised egg

implanting in the _____ . This is known as contraception.

Hormone-based contraceptives include oral contraceptives (the _____), implants, injections, and

patches. Spermicides kill _____ – this is a chemical method.

_____ methods prevent the sperm reaching the egg. Methods include _____ and

diaphragms. Other methods of contraception are intrauterine devices, _____ (not having sexual

intercourse), and surgical sterilisation.

B The contraceptive implant contains low doses of progesterone.

a Explain how it prevents pregnancy.

_____

_____

_____

b Give one advantage and one disadvantage of using this form of contraception.

Advantage _____

_____

Disadvantage _____

_____

C Use the chart opposite to answer the following questions:

a Name the non-hormonal contraceptive that has the lowest proportion of unexpected pregnancy.

_____

b Calculate the proportion of women who would **not** have an unexpected pregnancy using the rhythm method.

_____ %

c A group of 1500 women wishing to become pregnant used no contraception for a year.

Estimate the number who got pregnant.

Explain why this is not an accurate number.

_____

_____

_____

_____

_____

Bar chart: contraception type vs proportion of women with unexpected pregnancy in first year of use. Bars (top to bottom): IUD (levonorgestrel), IUD (copper T), patch, pill, diaphragm, condom, rhythm method, spermicides, no method. x-axis: 0% 10% 20% 30% 40% 50% 60% 70% 80% 90%. proportion of women with unexpected pregnancy in first year of use

B11.8 Infertility treatments

A Fill in the gaps to complete the sentences.

FSH and _____ can be used as a fertility drug to stimulate _____ in women with low FSH levels.

In vitro fertilisation (_____) uses FSH and LH to stimulate maturation of ova that are collected,

_____ , and allowed to start development before being placed in the _____ .

B IVF is a form of fertility treatment.

Describe the stages that take place during IVF.

_____

_____

_____

_____

_____

C 4248 babies were born as a result of IVF treatment.

1062 were multiple births (twins or triplets). The rest were single births.

Complete the pie chart below to show this data.

D There are many issues surrounding the use of IVF.

Write down:

a one ethical issue.

_____

b one economic issue.

_____

c one social issue.

_____

B11.9 Plant hormones and responses

A Fill in the gaps to complete the sentences.

Plants are sensitive to _____ and gravity. The responses to these stimuli are called tropisms and are the

result of the unequal distribution of _____ .

Shoots grow _____ light (phototropism) and against the force of _____ (gravitropism).

_____ grow in the direction of the force of gravity.

B Explain the function of tropisms in plants:

a Phototropism _____

_____

b Gravitropism _____

_____

_____

C A seedling is planted in the ground as shown in diagram **A**.

root   shoot

gravity   gravity

A   B

a Use a pen or pencil to shade in the region on each plant shoot where the levels of auxin are highest.

b On diagram **B**, draw the root and shoot of the seed after a few days.

D Explain why the shoot and root grow in this way.

Use what you know about the action of auxins.

_____

_____

_____

_____

B11.10 Using plant hormones

A Fill in the gaps to complete the sentences.

People have found ways of using plant hormones to help grow plants more successfully.

_____ are used as weed killers, _____ powders, and in tissue culture.

Ethene is used to control _____ ripening.

_____ can be used to increase fruit size, end seed _____, and promote flowering.

B Auxins stimulate growth in plants.

Explain:

a why spraying a plant with auxins will kill it.

_____

_____

b why farmers want to remove weeds from their crop fields.

_____

_____

c how spraying auxins in a wheat field will kill only the weeds, and not the wheat.

_____

C A hypothesis is 'using hormone rooting power on cuttings will increase growth'.

Plan an investigation to test this hypothesis. You should include:

- A simple method
- A prediction containing a scientific explanation

_____

_____

_____

_____

_____

_____

_____

_____

_____

_____

_____

_____

D Fruit growers pick their fruit and transport it when it is unripe.

a Explain why they do this.

_____

_____

b Describe how the fruit is ripened quickly for supply to shops.

_____

B11 Practice questions

01 **Figure 1** shows the male reproductive system.

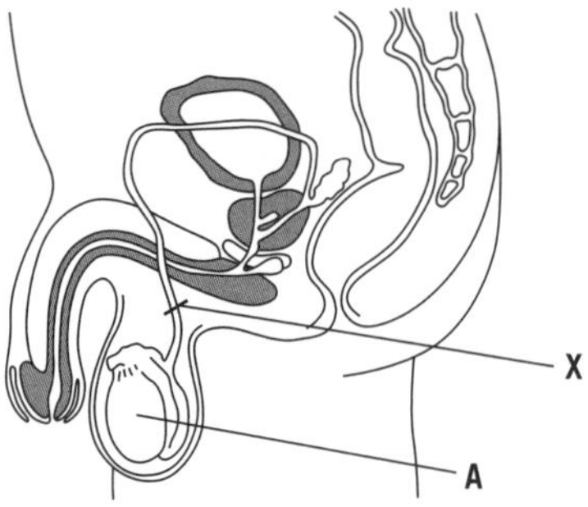

Figure 1

01.1 Name the structure labelled **A**.   [1 mark]
_____

01.2 This structure produces a hormone. Name the hormone and describe its functions.   [3 marks]
_____
_____
_____
_____

01.3 The man has had an operation where a tube is cut. The cut is labelled **X** in **Figure 1.**

Explain how this operation would prevent his partner from becoming pregnant.   [2 marks]
_____
_____
_____
_____

01.4 Evaluate the advantages and disadvantages of this operation as a form of contraception.   [4 marks]
_____
_____
_____
_____
_____
_____
_____
_____
_____

02 Paul is a professional footballer with a normal BMI. He has diabetes.

His diet can help control his blood glucose levels. He must also inject himself with insulin every day.

02.1 Give the type of diabetes Paul has.

Explain your answer.   [2 marks]
_____
_____
_____

02.2 Paul is playing a football match immediately after lunch.

Explain how this changes the amount of insulin he would need to inject.   [2 marks]
_____
_____
_____
_____

02.3 Suggest **two** reasons why insulin is injected, rather than taken as a tablet.   [2 marks]
_____
_____
_____
_____
_____
_____

B11 Checklist

	Student Book	😊	😐	😞
I can define the word hormone.	11.1			
I can identify the main organs of the endocrine system.	11.1			
I can describe the role of the pituitary gland.	11.1			
I can describe the role of the pancreas in monitoring and controlling blood glucose concentration.	11.2			
I can explain how insulin controls blood glucose levels in the body.	11.2			
I can describe how glucagon and insulin interact to control blood glucose levels in the body.	11.2			
I can explain what causes diabetes.	11.2			
I can describe the differences in the ways type 1 and type 2 diabetes are treated.	11.3			
I can describe what adrenaline and thyroxine do in the body.	11.4			
I can explain the importance of negative feedback systems.	11.4			
I can name the main human reproductive hormones.	11.5			
I can describe how hormones control the changes at puberty.	11.5			
I can describe the roles of hormones in human reproduction.	11.6			
I can explain how hormones interact to control the menstrual cycle.	11.6			
I can name methods of hormonal and non-hormonal contraception.	11.7			
I can explain how hormones can be used to treat infertility.	11.8			
I can describe how plants respond to light and gravity.	11.9			
I can explain the importance of auxin in plant responses.	11.9			
I can describe how plant hormones are used in agriculture and horticulture.	11.10			

B12.1 Controlling body temperature

A Fill in the gaps to complete the sentences.

Your body temperature is monitored and controlled by the thermoregulatory centre in your _____.

The _____ and thermoregulatory centre both contain _____ receptors.

If the body temperature is too high, blood vessels _____ (vasodilation) and sweat is produced from the

sweat glands. Both cause a transfer of _____ from the skin to the environment.

If the body temperature is too _____, blood vessels constrict (vasoconstriction) and _____

stops, reducing the rate of transfer of energy to the environment.

_____ also starts, which raises the temperature of the body due to respiration in the muscles.

B Bethany is outside on a hot day. Her core body temperature starts to rise above 37 °C.

a Explain why it is dangerous for her core body temperature to remain high for too long.

_____

_____

b Describe how the thermoregulatory centre in the brain detects a rise in core body temperature, and how it
coordinates a response.

_____

_____

_____

_____

c Name the **two** mechanisms used in order to bring her core body temperature back down to 37 °C.

1 _____ **2** _____

C These statements about thermoregulation are **incorrect.**

Write **correct** versions of them.

a Sweating cools down the body because sweat is cold.

_____

_____

b During vasoconstriction, blood capillaries in the skin constrict.

_____

_____

D Explain why your body temperature increases when you exercise.

_____

_____

_____

_____

B12.2 Removing waste products

A Fill in the gaps to complete the sentences.

Water leaves the body via the _____ during exhalation.

_____, mineral ions, and urea are lost through the skin in sweat.

There is no control over water, mineral ion, or urea loss by the lungs or skin.

Urea, along with excess water and _____ ions, is removed via the kidneys in the _____.
The loss of water and mineral ions is carefully balanced by the body.

B Your body produces carbon dioxide and urea as waste products.

Complete the table to describe where in the body they are produced and how

Waste product	Where in the body it is produced	How it is produced	How it is removed
urea			
carbon dioxide			

C Your body ensures that the concentration of mineral ions in the blood remains relatively constant.

a Explain why this is vital for healthy cell function.

_____

_____

_____

b Describe a controlled way of removing excess mineral ions from the body.

_____

c Give an uncontrolled way of removing excess mineral ions from the body.

_____

D The data in the table show the amount of water a person loses from different sources on a typical day.

Use the data to fill in the gaps in the sentences below.

a Calculate the total volume of water lost each day **in dm³**.

Source	Volume per day in cm³
urine	1500
skin	500
lungs	350
faeces	150

_____ dm³

b Calculate the percentage lost through the skin.

_____%

c It is a hot day, and Stefan has not drunk very much.

Describe how the volumes shown in the table would change.

_____

_____

B12.3 The human kidney

A Fill in the gaps to complete the sentences.

The kidneys are organs that are important for homeostasis, they have a role in controlling the _____ and mineral ion balance of your body.

A healthy kidney produces urine by _____ the blood. It then reabsorbs all of the glucose, plus any mineral ions and water needed by your body.

Excess mineral ions and _____, along with urea, form _____ which is stored in the bladder.

The water balance of the blood is maintained by the hormone _____, which changes the amount of water reabsorbed by the kidney _____.

B The diagram shows some of the organs in the body. Label it.

C The table below shows the concentration of substances in the blood and urine of a typical person.

Substance	Concentration in mg/100 cm³	
	In blood	In urine
urea	0.03	1.8
glucose	0.10	0.0
amino acids	0.05	0.0

a Describe the difference in concentration for urea and glucose.

Give a reason for each difference.

Urea _____

_____

Glucose _____

_____

b Calculate the mass of amino acids in 1 dm³ of blood.

_____

D Explain how ADH regulates the concentration of water in the blood.

_____

_____

_____

_____

_____

_____

A Fill in the gaps to complete the sentences.

People with kidney _____ may be treated by regular sessions on a kidney dialysis machine or by having a kidney transplant.

During a kidney _____ the failed kidneys are replaced with healthy ones from a donor.

During _____ the patient loses the excess _____ and mineral ions from their blood.

The levels of useful substances in the blood are kept _____ .

B Casey has kidney failure.

a Give **one** advantage of her having dialysis.

_____

_____

b Give **one** disadvantage of her having dialysis.

_____

_____

C The diagram below shows a patient having kidney dialysis.

Label it by writing **A**, **B**, **C**, **D**, or **E** in the right-hand column of the table below.

'dirty' blood (arterial blood)	
'clean' blood	
fresh dialysis fluid	
used dialysis fluid	
partially permeable membrane between blood and dialysis fluid	

D During dialysis, it is vital that patients lose waste substances but they do not lose useful substances from their blood.

a Give **one** example of each type of substance:

Waste product _____

Useful substance _____

b Explain how this is possible through the control of the dialysis fluid.

_____

_____

_____

_____

_____

B12.5 Kidney transplants

A Fill in the gaps to complete the sentences.

In a kidney transplant, a healthy kidney from a _____ replaces the function of the diseased or damaged kidney.

There is a risk of _____ because the _____ system of the patient will attack the donor kidney.

To try and prevent this, the _____ types of the donor and the recipient are matched as closely as possible. _____ drugs are also used.

B a Describe what happens during a kidney transplant.

_____

_____

b Explain why a kidney donor can be living, but a heart donor cannot.

_____

_____

C Describe the advantages and disadvantages of having a kidney transplant for someone with kidney failure.

Advantages

_____

_____

_____

Disadvantages

_____

_____

_____

D

Use the data in the graph to:

a Explain why there are many people in the UK waiting for a kidney transplant.

_____

_____

b Describe the trend.

_____

_____

B12 Practice questions

01 The human kidney removes urea from the blood.

Name **two** other substances removed from the blood by the kidney. [2 marks]

1 _____

2 _____

02 People with kidney failure cannot remove urea from their blood. They need kidney dialysis treatment. During dialysis, blood from a patient passes through a dialysis machine.

Figure 1 shows a diagram of what happens during dialysis.

blood with urea enters here — the cells in the blood are too big to get through the membrane — blood without urea leaves here

membrane which is a very fine filter

clean solution — small urea molecules get through the membrane into this solution — solution carries the colourless urea away

Figure 1

02.1 Give one way dialysis is similar to:

Diffusion [1 mark]

_____

Osmosis [1 mark]

_____

02.2 The dialysis fluid is changed regularly.

Suggest why this is important. [3 marks]

_____

_____

_____

_____

02.3 $550\,cm^3$ of blood flows through the machine is each minute.

Calculate how much blood, in dm^3, will flow through the machine in 4 hours.

Show your working. [2 marks]

_____ dm^3

02.4 Another function of dialysis is to maintain normal blood glucose concentration.

Suggest how the concentration of glucose in the dialysis fluid helps to maintain this. [3 marks]

_____

_____

_____

03 Kidney failure can also be treated by transplanting a healthy donor kidney into the patient.

Evaluate the use of dialysis compared with a kidney transplant. [5 marks]

_____

_____

_____

_____

_____

_____

_____

_____

_____

_____

_____

_____

B12 Checklist

	Student Book	☺	☺	☹
I can describe how the body monitors its temperature.	12.1			
I can describe how processes in the skin maintain a core body temperature.	12.1			
I can name some waste products produced by the body.	12.2			
I can describe how the body gets rid of waste products.	12.2			
I can describe why the kidneys are important and how they work.	12.3			
I can explain how ADH regulates water balance.	12.3			
I can explain how dialysis can be used to carry out the function of damaged kidneys.	12.4			
I can evaluate the advantages and disadvantages of dialysis.	12.4			
I can describe what is involved in a kidney transplant.	12.5			
I can describe some of the advantages and disadvantages of having a kidney transplant.	12.5			

B13.1 Types of reproduction

A Fill in the gaps to complete the sentences.

Asexual reproduction involves _____ parent. There is no joining (fusion) of _____ cells (gametes). The offspring are formed by mitosis so they are all genetically _____ to their parent and each other. They are clones.

Gametes are formed during a type of cell division called _____ . In _____ reproduction male and female gametes fuse. There is a mixing of genetic information that leads to _____ in the offspring.

B Compare asexual and sexual reproduction.

_____

_____

_____

_____

_____

_____

C Name the type of reproduction described in each example below:

a Yeast budding _____

b Formation of a human zygote _____

c Human skin cells multiplying _____

D Explain why:

a Offspring produced by asexual reproduction look identical to each their parent.

_____

_____

b Offspring produced by sexual reproduction look similar, but not identical, to both parents.

_____

_____

E Complete the table to show **one** advantage and disadvantage of each type of reproduction.

	Asexual reproduction	Sexual reproduction
Advantage		
Disadvantage		

B13.2 Cell division in sexual reproduction

A Fill in the gaps to complete the sentences.

Cells in the reproductive organs divide by _____ to form the gametes (sex cells).

Body cells have _____ sets of chromosomes, gametes have only one set.

In meiosis, the genetic material is copied and then the cell _____ twice to form _____ genetically different gametes, each with a single set of chromosomes.

Gametes join at _____ to form a cell with the normal number of chromosomes. The new cell divides by _____ . The number of cells increases and as the embryo develops, the cells differentiate.

B Write the word being defined:

a Cell division that produces identical cells _____

b Cell division that produces gametes _____

c The joining of a male and female sex cell _____

d A fertilised egg _____

C The diagram below shows the process of meiosis.

Draw the correct number of chromosomes in each cell. The first one has been done for you.

A cell in the reproductive organs looks just like a normal body cell before it starts to divide and form gametes

As in normal cell division, the first step is that the chromosomes are copied

The cell divides in two, and these new cells immediately divide again

This gives four sex cells, each with a single set of chromosomes – in this case two instead of the original four

D Write the correct number of chromosomes in each of the following human cells.

skin cell _____

sperm cell _____

zygote _____

egg cell _____

ovary cell _____

B13.3 The best of both worlds

A Fill in the gaps to complete the sentences.

Sexual reproduction produces variation that helps survival through _____ selection if the environment changes. Natural selection is sped up by humans in _____ breeding.

_____ reproduction needs only one parent, it is often faster than sexual reproduction, and many identical offspring are produced when conditions are favourable.

Some organisms depend on _____ asexual and sexual reproduction depending on the circumstances.

Malaria parasites reproduce _____ in mosquitoes and asexually in their _____ host.

Many fungi reproduce asexually by _____ but can also reproduce sexually to give variation.

Many plants produce _____ sexually but also reproduce asexually, for example by _____ or bulb division.

B Compare sexual and asexual reproduction.

_____

_____

_____

_____

C Describe the advantages and disadvantages of sexual and asexual reproduction.

_____

_____

_____

_____

_____

_____

_____

_____

_____

D Strawberry plants can reproduce both sexually and asexually.

a Describe how they reproduce sexually.

_____

_____

b Describe how they reproduce asexually.

_____

_____

c Give **one** reason why it is an advantage to a strawberry plant to be able to use both forms of reproduction.

_____

_____

B13.4 DNA and the genome

A Fill in the gaps to complete the sentences.

The genetic material in the nucleus of a cell is composed of DNA. DNA is a _____ made up of two

strands forming a _____ helix.

A gene is a small section of DNA on a _____ . Each gene codes for a particular sequence of amino acids,

to make a specific _____ .

The _____ of an organism is the entire genetic material of that organism. The whole human genome

has now been studied and this will have great importance for medicine in the future.

B Define the term 'genome'.

_____

C Identify the parts labelled **W**, **X**, **Y**, and **Z** on the diagram:

W _____   X _____

Y _____   Z _____

D The 100 000 genomes project is a new research project being carried out in the UK.

Scientists will sequence the genome of patients with rare diseases and two of their closest relatives (such as their parents), who may or may not have the disease.

Suggest how the data from the project will help:

a to identify which rare diseases are inherited.

_____

_____

_____

_____

_____

b to develop treatments for rare diseases.

_____

_____

_____

B13.5 DNA structure and protein synthesis

A Fill in the gaps to complete the sentences.

The long strands of DNA consist of alternating _____ and phosphate sections. Attached to each sugar is

one of four bases – A, C, _____, or T.

Each unit of a sugar, phosphate, and base is known as a _____.

A sequence of _____ bases is the code for a particular amino acid.

The order of bases controls the order in which amino acids are assembled to produce a particular _____.

_____ molecules bring specific amino acids to add to the growing protein chain in the correct order.

B The diagram shows a short section of DNA.

Label one of each of the following structures:

phosphate   sugar   base   nucleotide

C The diagram below shows the bases on one strand of DNA.

Underneath each base, write the missing base on the complementary strand.

A	C	C	G	T	T	A

D A gene is a code for a protein.

Describe how the DNA code in a gene gets translated into a protein.

You should include how the order of amino acids is determined.

_____

_____

_____

_____

_____

B13.6 Gene expression and mutation

A Fill in the gaps to complete the sentences.

Not all parts of the DNA code for _____. Non-coding parts switch _____ on or off, so variations in these areas of DNA can affect how genes are _____.

A change in the DNA structure is a mutation. Most mutations do not alter the protein, or they alter it so slightly that the _____ is not affected.

A few mutations code for an altered protein with a different _____, affecting the function. This may be an advantage or a disadvantage.

B Define each of these terms:

a Non-coding DNA

_____

b Gene expression

_____

c Mutation

_____

C When a boy reaches puberty cells in his testes will start producing the hormone testosterone.

Explain what change happens in the DNA of the testes cells so they start producing testosterone.

_____

_____

_____

D Myostatin is a protein produced by muscle cells. Its function is to inhibit muscle cell growth.

a Suggest why animals with a mutation in the myostatin gene have larger muscles.

_____

_____

_____

b Explain why this could be an advantage.

_____

_____

_____

B13.7 Inheritance in action

A Fill in the gaps to complete the sentences.

Some characteristics are controlled by a single gene. Each gene may have different forms called _____ .

The _____ is the alleles present (e.g., BB). The _____ describes a trait (e.g., black fur).

If the two alleles are the _____ , the individual is homozygous for that trait. If the alleles are different,

the individual is _____ . A _____ allele, shown as a capital letter, is always expressed in

the phenotype, even if only one copy is present. A _____ allele, shown as a lower case letter, is only

expressed if _____ copies are present. Most characteristics are the result of multiple genes interacting,

rather than a single gene.

B The hair of a guinea pig may be straight or curly.

The allele for curly hair is dominant (H). The allele for straight hair is recessive (h).

Write down:

a a heterozygous genotype for hair type _____

b a homozygous dominant genotype for hair type _____

c the genotype for a guinea pig with straight hair _____

d all the possible genotypes for a guinea pig with curly hair _____

C Flower colour in a plant is inherited. White flowers is a recessive allele (t), yellow flowers is dominant (T).

a Plant 1 with genotype tt breeds with plant 2 which is homozygous dominant for flower colour.

Give the **phenotypes** of the two plants:

Plant 1 _____

Plant 2 _____

b Complete the Punnett square below to show the genotypes of offspring from the plants.

	Plant 1	
	t	t
Plant 2 T		
T		

c Give the phenotype of the offspring. _____

D Two of the offspring from activity **C** are bred together.

Draw a Punnett square in the space below to show this cross.

B13.8 More about genetics

A Fill in the gaps to complete the sentences.

_____ squares and family trees are used to show genetic crosses. They show the possible genotypes

and _____ of offspring. Direct proportion and _____ can be used to express the outcome

of a genetic cross.

Ordinary human body cells contain _____ pairs of chromosomes. 22 control general body

characteristics. The _____ chromosomes carry the genes that determine sex. Human females have two

_____ chromosomes. In _____ the sex chromosomes are different (XY).

B Fruit flies can have red eyes (E) or orange eyes (e).

The genetic cross opposite shows the possible offspring between two fruit flies.

Use the genetic cross to answer the following questions:

Gametes	E	e
E	EE	Ee
e	Ee	ee

a What colour eyes do the parents have? _____

b What proportion of the offspring have orange eyes? _____

c What proportion of the offspring are homozygous for eye colour? _____

d What is the ratio of red eyed to orange eyed offspring? _____

e What is the ratio of heterozygous to homozygous genotypes in the offspring? _____

C Human sex chromosomes are X and Y.

Complete the Punnett Square to show how sex is inherited.

Use it to explain why the ratio of men and women in the world is approximately 1:1.

	Mother	
Father		

_____

_____

D Earlobes can be attached to the head or free.

The diagram opposite shows a family tree.

Having attached earlobes may be caused by a recessive allele.
How does the family tree provide evidence for this?

_____

_____

_____

_____

■ male with free earlobes   ● female with free earlobes

□ male with attached earlobes   ○ female with attached earlobes

_____

_____

B13.9 Inherited disorders

A Fill in the gaps to complete the sentences.

Some disorders are caused by a change in the DNA. They can be passed from parent to child. These are

_____ disorders.

If a person has _____ they are born with extra fingers or toes. It is a dominant phenotype caused

by a _____ allele that can be inherited from either or both parents.

Cystic fibrosis causes thick _____ to build up in the lungs and the digestive and reproductive systems.

It is a recessive phenotype and is caused by _____ alleles that must be inherited from _____

parents.

B Complete the table to show information about two inherited disorders.

Inherited disorder	How it affects the body	Caused by inheriting: (tick the correct box)	
		One dominant allele	Two recessive alleles
Cystic fibrosis			
Polydactyly			

C Polydactyly is an inherited condition.

a Complete the Punnett square to show the genotypes of offspring between a mother who has polydactyly and a father who doesn't.

		Mother	
		D	d
Father	d		
	d		

b A student suggests 'if these parents have 4 children then 2 of them will definitely have polydactyly'.

Are they correct? Give a reason for your answer.

_____

_____

D Steven and Lucy do not have cystic fibrosis, but their daughter Maddy does.

a Explain how this is possible.

_____

_____

b They decide to have another child.

What is the probability that the child will have cystic fibrosis?

_____

B13.10 Screening for genetic disorders

A Fill in the gaps to complete the sentences.

Cells from embryos and _____ can be screened during pregnancy for the _____ that

cause many genetic disorders. The main methods for taking the cells include amniocentesis and chorionic

_____ sampling. Both have a risk of _____ .

Some couples may decide to use _____ to create embryos outside the body. These are then tested

before being implanted into the mother, so only babies without the disorder are born.

Screening raises economic, social, and _____ issues.

B To carry out screening, cells need to be tested. There are two main methods used to take cells from the developing baby. These are shown in the diagrams opposite.

Compare the two methods.

_____

_____

_____

_____

_____

_____

chorionic villus sampling – transabdominal method

needle

placenta

amniocentesis

needle

amniotic fluid

C Darvesh and Amita have a son with an inherited condition called beta thalassemia.

They wish to have another child who is not affected with the condition.

One option is for them to use IVF and screen the embryos.

a Describe the stages in this process.

_____

_____

_____

_____

b Give an ethical objection to the process.

_____

_____

B13 Practice questions

01 Connor has cystic fibrosis. Hannah is a carrier for the disease. Hannah and Connor are considering having a child together.

01.1 These are some of the questions that they could consider before making their decision.

A	Could we afford to have a child with cystic fibrosis?
B	What is the chance of us having a child with cystic fibrosis?
C	Shall we screen the fetus before it is born to see if it has cystic fibrosis?
D	If we do find out the fetus has cystic fibrosis should we have a termination?
E	Should we discuss this with a genetic counsellor?

Which question, **A**, **B**, **C**, **D**, or **E** is an economic consideration?

_____

Which question **A**, **B**, **C**, **D**, or **E** is an ethical issue?

_____

Which question **A**, **B**, **C**, **D**, or **E** can be answered by science? [3 marks]

_____

01.2 Calculate the probability that the fetus would have cystic fibrosis.

Use a Punnett square to help you.

Use **F** to represent the dominant allele and **f** to represent the recessive allele. [3 marks]

probability of fetus having cystic fibrosis _____

01.3 Connor and Hannah decide to have a baby. If Hannah becomes pregnant, they can use genetic screening to test the fetus for cystic fibrosis before it is born.

Describe the implications that need to be considered before using genetic screening.

[6 marks]

_____

_____

_____

_____

_____

_____

_____

_____

_____

_____

_____

_____

02 In 1986 there was an explosion at a nuclear power plant in Chernobyl, Ukraine.

Many of the people living nearby developed illnesses because of the release of radioactive materials into the atmosphere. These illnesses were caused by changes to DNA in body cells.

Suggest why changes to DNA may cause illnesses.

[4 marks]

_____

_____

_____

_____

_____

B13 Checklist

	Student Book	☺	😐	☹
I can describe the main differences between asexual and sexual reproduction.	13.1			
I can describe how cells divide by meiosis to form gametes.	13.2			
I can describe how meiosis halves the number of chromosomes in gametes and fertilisation restores the full number.	13.2			
I can explain how sexual reproduction gives rise to variation.	13.2			
I can describe the advantages and disadvantages of asexual and sexual reproduction.	13.3			
I can describe how some organisms reproduce both asexually and sexually depending on the circumstances.	13.3			
I can describe how DNA is the material of inheritance.	13.4			
I can define the term genome.	13.4			
I can outline some of the benefits of studying the human genome.	13.4			
I can describe how the structure of DNA relates to its function.	13.5			
I can explain how DNA controls protein synthesis.	13.5			
I can describe what happens in mutations.	13.6			
I can describe how genes are expressed.	13.6			
I can identify different forms of genes, called alleles, as either dominant or recessive.	13.7			
I can predict the results of genetic crosses when a characteristic is controlled by a single gene.	13.7			
I can construct Punnett square diagrams.	13.7			
I can interpret Punnett square diagrams.	13.7			
I can use proportion and ratios to express the outcome of a genetic cross.	13.8			
I can describe how sex is inherited.	13.8			
I can interpret a family tree.	13.8			
I can describe how the human genetic disorders polydactyly and cystic fibrosis are inherited.	13.9			
I can recall that embryos are screened for some of the alleles that cause genetic disorders.	13.10			
I can explain some of the concerns and issues associated with these screening processes.	13.10			

B14.1 Variation

A Fill in the gaps to complete the sentences.

_____ is the differences in the characteristics of individuals in a population. It may be due to differences

in the _____ inherited from parents (genetic causes), the conditions in which organisms develop

(_____ causes), or a combination of _____ .

Studying identical _____ helps scientists to understand what controls different characteristics.

If a characteristic is very similar in identical twins, then it is more likely to be caused by _____ .

If a characteristic is very different, it is more likely to be influenced by the _____ .

B Fill in the table to give the examples of variation mentioned in the description below.

Amelie has short brown hair, green eyes, and a small scar just above her right eyebrow. She speaks English with a French accent. In fact, she speaks many languages and has a high IQ. She is 153 cm tall and has a mass of 58 kg. Her blood group is A.

Variation due to just genetics	Variation due to just the environment	Variation due to a combination of genetics and the environment
1	1	1
	2	
2	3	2
	4	
3	5	3

C A student wanted to investigate how the environment affected variation in plants.

They planned to use seedlings with identical genes and grow them in different environmental conditions.

a Give **three** independent variables that they could study.

1 _____

2 _____

3 _____

b Suggest a suitable dependent variable they could use.

_____

D A scientist carried out a study. His hypothesis was: 'Type 1 diabetes is caused only by genetics.'

He studied identical twins. In 85% of the pairs of twins studied, if one twin had type 1 diabetes then the other twin also had diabetes.

a Does this evidence support his hypothesis? _____

b Explain your answer.

_____

_____

_____

B14.2 Evolution by natural selection

A Fill in the gaps to complete the sentences.

The theory of evolution by _____ selection states that all species of living things have evolved from

simple life forms that first developed over 3 _____ years ago.

Changes in the DNA are called _____ . They occur continuously. Very rarely this leads to a new

phenotype. This may form individuals that are more suited to an _____ change. They are likely to

survive and _____ successfully. These alleles are then passed on to the next generation. This can lead to

a relatively rapid change in the species.

If two populations of a species become so different that they can no longer interbreed to produce _____

offspring, they have formed two new _____ .

B Describe what a mutation is.

_____

C One example of natural selection is the increase in bacteria that are resistant to antibiotics.

Explain how this happens. Use the stages of natural selection as shown below.

Mutation of a gene _____

_____

Advantage to survival _____

_____

Breed _____

_____

Pass on genes _____

_____

D In a population of mice, some individuals have a mutation that gives
them slightly better eyesight than the others.

a Explain how this gives them a better chance of survival.

_____

_____

_____

b Explain why this means that the quality of eyesight in the whole population of mice will slowly improve.

_____

_____

_____

B14.3 Selective breeding

A Fill in the gaps to complete the sentences.

In selective breeding, humans select plants and _____ with desired characteristics to _____

together. Desired characteristics include: disease _____ in food crops, increased food production in

animals and plants, domestic dogs with a _____ nature, and heavily scented _____ .

Problems can occur with selective breeding, including defects in some animals due to lack of _____ .

B Wheat is an important food crop that is grown on farms.

Give **two** useful characteristics of wheat.

1 _____

_____

2 _____

_____

C Greyhounds are dogs used for racing.

A greyhound breeder wants to use selective breeding to create a very fast dog.

a Describe the steps he should carry out in order to do this.

_____

_____

_____

_____

_____

_____

_____

D Inbreeding is an issue that the dog breeder in activity **C** should be aware of.

a Describe what inbreeding means.

_____

b Explain why the breeder should be careful it does not occur.

_____

_____

_____

B14.4 Genetic engineering

A Fill in the gaps to complete the sentences.

Genetic _____ involves modifying (changing) the genetic material of an organism to give the genetically

engineered organism a new, desirable characteristic.

_____ from the chromosomes of humans and other organisms can be 'cut out' using _____

and transferred to the cells of bacteria and other organisms using a _____ , which is usually a bacterial

plasmid or a virus.

Plant crops have been genetically engineered to be _____ to certain pesticides and diseases, or to

produce bigger fruits. These are called genetically _____ (GM) crops.

B Genetically engineered bacteria and fungi can be used to produce useful proteins from other organisms.

The diagram shows how bacteria are used to produce human insulin.

a Describe what is happening at each stage.

V _____

W _____

X _____

Y _____

Z _____

b Name the vector in this process. _____

C As the human population of the world increases, it is important to increase the amount of food produced.

Explain how genetic engineering could help to increase crop yields.

_____

_____

_____

_____

_____

D In the USA, 158 million hectares of land is taken up growing maize. 58 million acres of this is GM maize.

Calculate the percentage of land used to grow GM maize.

_____

B14.5 Cloning

A Fill in the gaps to complete the sentences.

A clone is an individual which has been produced asexually and is genetically _____ to the parent.

Plants can be cloned using _____ culture or taking _____.

Embryos can be cloned. This involves splitting apart cells from a developing animal _____ before they

become _____ and then transplanting the identical embryos into host mothers.

B Both taking cuttings and tissue culture can be used to clone plants.

a Give **one** advantage of using tissue culture rather than taking cuttings.

_____

b Give **one** disadvantage of using tissue culture rather than taking cuttings.

_____

C The diagram below shows how cattle embryos are cloned.

a Use the diagram to describe how the process is carried out.

_____

_____

_____

_____

_____

_____

_____

_____

_____

_____

_____

early embryo (cluster of identical cells)

b Explain why each calf born is a clone.

_____

_____

D There are many issues surrounding embryo cloning.

a Describe **one** economic reason why farmers use embryo cloning.

_____

_____

_____

b Describe **one** ethical concern that people have about embryo cloning.

_____

_____

_____

B14.6 Adult cell cloning

A Fill in the gaps to complete the sentences.

Adult cell _____ involves taking a cell from an adult animal and making an embryo that contains the

_____ genetic information as the adult cell. When the embryo has developed into a ball of cells, it is

inserted into the _____ of an adult female to continue its development.

B In 1996, Dolly the sheep was the first large mammal to be cloned using adult cell cloning.

The diagram below shows how the procedure was carried out.

adult cell
(e.g., skin,
udder)

mature
egg

Use the diagram to describe how adult cell cloning is carried out.

_____

_____

_____

_____

_____

C A farmer has an award-winning cow. He wants to use her to produce many award-winning calves.

Explain why he would prefer to use adult cell cloning, rather than embryo cloning, to achieve this.

_____

_____

_____

D Scientists are considering using adult cell cloning to create populations of clones of extinct animals. These could
then be released into the wild.

Suggest drawbacks of using this technique.

_____

_____

_____

_____

_____

_____

B14.7 Ethics of genetic technologies

A Fill in the gaps to complete the sentences.

Scientists are exploring the use of genetic modification to put 'healthy' genes into affected cells and overcome some

_____ disorders.

There are _____ and risks associated with genetic engineering in agriculture and medicine.

One benefit is that growing GM crops can _____ food production.

One _____ is that genes from GM crops might spread to wildlife.

Some people are worried about genetic engineering being used to create _____ babies with particular

characteristics such as high intelligence. These are ethical objections.

B Genetic engineering is used to produce genetically modified crops.

Many people in the UK are against growing genetically modified crops.

a Describe their concerns.

_____

_____

_____

_____

b An example of a use of genetic engineering is the production of golden rice.

Golden rice has a gene inserted into it so it produces vitamin A.

White rice does not contain any vitamin A.

Countries where people eat mainly white rice have high levels of blindness due to a lack of vitamin A.

Suggest why people in these countries may be more in favour of growing genetically modified crops than people
who live in the UK.

_____

_____

_____

C Genetic engineering could be used to cure illnesses.

a Name this form of treatment. _____

b Name one disorder that could be cured in this way. _____

c Suggest how it could be carried out.

_____

_____

_____

_____

B14 Practice questions

01 A student carried out a survey in her local town centre.

She asked people if they were concerned about growing GM (genetically modified) crops in the UK.

01.1 Describe the difference between a normal crop and a GM crop. [1 mark]

_____

_____

01.2 She started to plot her results as a bar chart, shown in **Figure 1**.

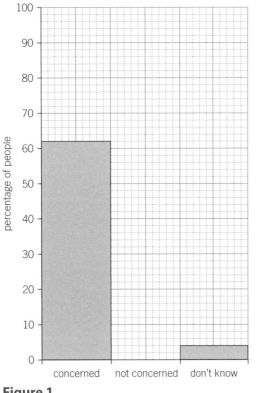

Figure 1

Calculate the percentage of people who were not concerned about GM crops. [2 marks]

_____%

01.3 Show your answer to **01.2** on the bar chart. [1 mark]

01.4 Give **two** reasons why some people are concerned about growing GM crops. [2 marks]

1 _____

_____

2 _____

_____

02 The processes of natural selection and selective breeding have both contributed to the huge variation of life on Earth.

Compare natural selection and selective breeding. Include the similarities and differences between them. [6 marks]

_____

_____

_____

_____

_____

_____

_____

_____

_____

_____

_____

_____

_____

_____

_____

_____

_____

B14 Checklist

	Student Book	☺	☺	☹
I can explain what makes someone different from the rest of their family.	14.1			
I can explain why identical twins are not exactly the same in every way.	14.1			
I can describe how natural selection works.	14.2			
I can explain how evolution occurs via natural selection.	14.2			
I can define selective breeding.	14.3			
I can describe how selective breeding works.	14.3			
I can evaluate selective breeding by considering the benefits and risks.	14.3			
I can evaluate the potential benefits and problems associated with genetic engineering in agriculture and medicine.	14.4			
I can describe how genes are transferred from one organism to another in genetic engineering to obtain a desired characteristic.	14.4			
I can describe different ways of creating clones.	14.5			
I can describe why clones are useful.	14.5			
I can describe how adult cell cloning is carried out.	14.6			
I can explain the benefits and risks of adult cell cloning.	14.6			
I can explain some of the concerns and uncertainties about the new genetic technologies, such as cloning and genetic engineering.	14.7			

B15.1 The history of genetics

A Fill in the gaps to complete the sentences.

Gregor _____ carried out breeding experiments on _____. He concluded that inheritance is determined by 'units' that are passed on.

In the early 20th century, it was observed that chromosomes and 'units' behaved in similar ways. This led to the idea that the units, now called _____, were located on the chromosomes.

In the mid-20th century, the structure of _____ was determined and the mechanism of gene function was worked out.

B Gregor Mendel was a monk who lived in the mid-19th century. He carried out breeding experiments on pea plants.

He bred tall plants (T) with short plants (t). He found that 100% of the offspring were tall.

a Draw a Punnett square to show this cross.

b He then bred the offspring of this cross together.

Predict what the ratio of tall plants to small plants would be.

You can use a Punnett square to help you.

_____

C Mendel kept records of everything he did, and analysed his results.

a What did Mendel do with the records of his results that was unusual for that time?

_____

_____

b Why did people not accept his theories until 16 years after his death?

_____

_____

_____

D Gene theory has now been accepted. It explains how genes have an effect on an organism.

a Explain why it took several years to develop gene theory.

_____

_____

b Gene theory could change in the future. Explain why.

_____

_____

B15.2 Theories of evolution

A Fill in the gaps to complete the sentences.

The theory of evolution proposed by Jean-Baptiste _____ was based on the idea that changes that occur in an organism during its lifetime can be inherited.

Charles _____ proposed his theory of evolution by _____ selection, largely as a result of observations made on a round the world expedition.

Individual organisms in a particular species show _____.

_____ always gives more offspring than the _____ can support. The organisms that have inherited the characteristics most suited to their environment – the 'fittest' – are more likely to _____ and breed successfully.

When they breed, they pass on these characteristics to their _____.

B Over time, giraffes have evolved to have longer necks.

a Describe how Lamarck's theory of evolution explained how giraffe's necks got longer.

_____

_____

b Suggest **one** reason why we no longer accept this theory for the great majority of inheritance.

_____

_____

C Charles Darwin proposed the theory of natural selection to explain how evolution happens.

a Giraffes eat leaves from trees.

Use this information to explain one way that giraffes could have evolved to have long necks via **natural selection.**

_____

_____

_____

_____

b More recently, scientists have proposed another way that the long necks of giraffes evolved by natural selection.

They observed that male giraffes use their necks to fight each other for a mate.

They discovered that longer a giraffe's neck, the more successful they are in a fight.

Use this information to explain another way that giraffes could have evolved to have long necks via **natural selection.**

_____

_____

_____

c Suggest why scientists cannot be sure how giraffes' long necks evolved.

_____

_____

B15.3 Accepting Darwin's ideas

A Fill in the gaps to complete the sentences.

Darwin's theory of evolution by _____ selection was only gradually accepted for a number of reasons.

These include:

- Conflict with the widely held _____ that God made all the animals and plants on Earth

- Insufficient _____

- No mechanism for explaining variation and _____.

B Charles Darwin collected evidence to support his theory of natural selection.

Explain why he needed evidence.

_____

C The Galapagos Islands are a group of islands found off the coast of South America.

Darwin noticed that the finches living on the different islands had slightly different beaks to each other.

The diagram below shows three of the finches he studied, **A**, **B**, and **C**. Each lives on a different island.

A   B   C

a Each finch is adapted to living in its habitat. Explain how the beaks show this.

_____
_____

b Use the theory of natural selection to explain how the long beak of finch **C** evolved from finches with shorter beaks.

_____
_____
_____
_____

D Darwin published his theory in 1859.

a What pushed Darwin to publish his theory earlier than he wished?

_____

b Explain why many scientists did not accept his theory when it was first published.

_____
_____
_____
_____

c Explain why scientists accept Darwin's theory now.

_____
_____
_____

B15.4 Evolution and speciation

A Fill in the gaps to complete the sentences.

Alfred Russel _____ independently proposed the theory of _____ by natural selection. Wallace worked worldwide gathering evidence for evolutionary theory. He is best known for his work on his theory of _____. This explains how new species arise as a result of _____ to create two populations. Natural selection operates differently on them so the populations become so different that successful _____ is no longer possible.

B Poison dart frogs have colourful markings on their skin, called warning colouration.

In 1867, in a letter to Darwin, Wallace described warning colouration as clear evidence of natural selection at work.

a Explain what the colouring of the poison dart frog signifies.

_____

b Suggest how this is evidence for natural selection.

_____

_____

_____

C Originally only one squirrel species inhabited the forests around the Grand Canyon in the USA.

About 10 000 years ago, when the last ice age ended, the canyon changed in a way that blocked the movement of squirrels across it.

The species evolved into two new species of squirrel on either side of the canyon: the Abert and the Kaibab tassel-eared squirrels.

a Name:

The process by which a new species arises _____

The type of isolation created by the change in the canyon _____

b Describe why the two populations are defined as different species.

_____

c Explain why the two new species evolved.

_____

_____

_____

B15.5 Evidence for evolution

A Fill in the gaps to complete the sentences.

Fossils are the remains of organisms from _____ of years ago that can be found in _____ ,

ice, and other places. They may be formed in different ways including being preserved so they do not

_____ , parts being replaced by _____ as they decay, and as preserved traces of organisms

such as footprints.

Fossils help us build up a picture of life on Earth long ago. But scientists cannot be certain how _____

on Earth started. The fossil record is not complete for several reasons:

- Early forms of life were _____ -bodied so left few traces behind.

- The right conditions for fossil formation were rare.

- Many fossils have been destroyed by _____ activity, such as volcanoes.

- Not all fossils have been found.

B Fossils are good evidence for the theory of evolution by natural selection.

a Name the scientist who proposed this theory.

_____

b Describe how fossils help support the theory of evolution.

_____

_____

c Describe one reason why fossils are limited in what they can tell us about how life on Earth has evolved.

_____

_____

C Many fossils found in rocks are formed when animal bones are replaced by minerals.

Describe how this process takes place.

_____

_____

_____

D The timescales we use when talking about evolution are very large so we use standard form.

Complete the table to show the timescales in standard form.

Timescale	Standard form
10 000 years	
	1×10^9 years
100 million years	
	1×10^6 years

B15.6 Fossils and extinction

A Fill in the gaps to complete the sentences.

You can learn from _____ how much or how little organisms have changed as life has developed on Earth.

_____ is the permanent loss of all members of a _____. It may be caused by a number of factors including a change in temperature, new _____ that can wipe out prey animals, new diseases, or new, more successful competitors.

B Modern day crocodiles are very similar to their ancestors who lived millions of years ago.

a What evidence do we have for this?

_____

_____

b Use what you know about evolution to suggest a reason why they have not changed.

_____

_____

C The baiji is a species of dolphin found only in the Yangtze River in China.

The river travels through many industrial and residential areas. It is used extensively for fishing.

An expedition in 2006 failed to find any baiji in the river. It is thought to be extinct.

a Suggest possible causes for the extinction of the baiji.

_____

_____

_____

b Explain why scientists are not certain that it is extinct.

_____

_____

D The bar graph opposite shows the number of animal extinctions that took place from the 17th century to the 20th century.

a Describe the trend in the graph.

_____

_____

b Suggest **one** reason for this.

_____

_____

B15.7 More about extinction

A Fill in the gaps to complete the sentences.

Extinction can be caused by a variety of factors including changes to the environment over geological time and

single catastrophic events, such as massive _____ eruptions or collisions with _____ .

During a _____ extinction, many of the species on Earth die out. The last mass extinction was when the

_____ became extinct around 65 million years ago. Scientists have presented different theories for why

this happened, with _____ to support them.

B Give **two** changes that could cause a mass extinction event.

1 _____

2 _____

C Some scientists think that a giant asteroid collided with the Earth 65 million years ago.

Explain why this could have caused the dinosaurs to become extinct.

_____

_____

_____

_____

D Other scientists have proposed a different theory for how the dinosaurs became extinct. They suggest that global
temperatures decreased and the extinction happened very slowly.

a For each piece of evidence (**V–Z**), tick a box to show what theory it supports.

Evidence	✓ if it supports the asteroid collision theory	✓ if it supports the decrease in temperature theory
V. Unexpected changes to fossils in Norway		
W. Huge crater in Chicxulub, Mexico		
X. Layers of crater debris in rocks that are 65 million years old		
Y. The fossil record shows tropical vegetation was replaced by woodland plants		
Z. The Manicouagan crater in Canada was formed by a huge asteroid. However, no mass extinction took place at this time.		

b Explain why the asteroid collision is the most widely accepted theory.

_____

_____

_____

B15.8 Antibiotic-resistant bacteria

A Fill in the gaps to complete the sentences.

Bacteria can evolve quickly because they _____ at a fast rate. Mutations can produce strains of bacteria

that are resistant to _____ and so are not killed. An example is _____ . Resistant strains

survive and reproduce, so the population _____ by natural selection. The strain will then spread

because people are not immune to it and there is no effective treatment.

To reduce the rate of development of antibiotic resistant strains, it is important that _____ only prescribe

antibiotics when they need to, and patients use the antibiotics as prescribed and complete each course. The use of

antibiotics on farms should also be restricted. Scientists are developing new antibiotics but this is _____

and slow.

B A person gets infected with bacteria. They take antibiotics.

Complete the diagram sequence to show how a strain of antibiotic-resistant bacteria could appear.

Use the representations in the diagram key.

A chance mutation
makes some individual
bacteria resistant to the
antibiotic.

The antibiotic kills the
non-resistant bacteria.

The resistant bacteria
survive and reproduce.

key

antibiotic resistant
bacteria

killed bacteria

C Study the bar chart opposite.

Draw **two** conclusions from the data.

1 _____

_____

2 _____

_____

D There are several ways to stop the development of more strains of
antibiotic-resistant bacteria.

For each person below, suggest one thing they can do to help.

a A person visiting a sick relative in a hospital

_____

b A nurse working in a hospital

_____

c A GP who prescribes drugs

_____

d A person who has been given antibiotics

_____

B15.9 Classification

A Fill in the gaps to complete the sentences.

Carl _____ classified organisms into groups based on their features. Organisms are named using the

_____ system of genus and species.

As _____ improved, scientists had new evidence of the internal structures of organisms.

Our understanding of genomes also improved. These developments led scientists to propose new

models of _____ .

B Living things are classified into groups.

Write in the missing classification groups. They are in order of size, largest first.

_____ → Phylum → Class → Order → Family → Genus → _____

C Compare the major features of organisms from the plant and animal kingdom.

_____

_____

_____

_____

D The polar bear has the scientific name *Ursus maritimus.*

Write the polar bear's:

a Kingdom _____

b Species _____

c Genus _____

B15.10 New systems of classification

A Fill in the gaps to complete the sentences.

A domain is a new, higher level of classification above _____ .

Studying the similarities and differences between organisms allows us to classify them into the domains

archaea, _____ , and eukaryota.

Classification helps us to understand evolutionary and ecological relationships.

Models such as evolutionary _____ allow us to suggest relationships between organisms.

B Work from scientists such as Carl Woese has resulted in the introduction of a new system of classification.

Write these words in the correct boxes on the diagram to show how living things are now classified.

| plants | archaebacteria | bacteria |
| domain | protista | eukaryota |

```
┌──────────────┐   ┌──────────────┐
│              │   │   kingdom    │
└──────────────┘   └──────────────┘
┌──────────────┐   ┌──────────────┐
│   archaea    │───│              │
└──────────────┘   └──────────────┘

┌──────────────┐   ┌──────────────┐
│              │───│  eubacteria  │
└──────────────┘   └──────────────┘

                   ┌──────────────┐
                   │   animals    │
                   └──────────────┘
┌──────────────┐   ┌──────────────┐
│              │◄──│              │
└──────────────┘   └──────────────┘
                   ┌──────────────┐
                   │    fungi     │
                   └──────────────┘
                   ┌──────────────┐
                   │              │
                   └──────────────┘
```

C A scientist uses a microscope to study a unicellular organism.

A labelled image of what they see is shown opposite.

a Name the domain that the organism belongs to.

_____

b Explain the reason for your answer.

_____

_____

nucleus

contractile vacuole

D The diagram opposite shows an evolutionary tree.

Use the information in the diagram to answer the following questions:

a How long ago did the common ancestor of the chimp and lizard exist on Earth?

_____

_____

common ancestor

200 million years ago

5 million years ago

b Suggest why humans, chimps, and lizards all have four limbs.

_____

c Explain why the following statement is incorrect: 'Humans evolved from chimps.'

_____

_____

B15 Practice questions

01 Red squirrels (*Sciurus vulgaris*) live in forests in the UK.

They were common in the UK until a different species, the grey squirrel (*Sciurus carolinensis*), was introduced from America in 1876.

01.1 Name the genus that both squirrels belong to.

[1 mark]

_____

01.2 Predict whether red and grey squirrels can breed to produce fertile offspring.

Give a reason for your answer. [2 marks]

_____

_____

_____

01.3 Since the introduction of grey squirrels, the population of red squirrels in the UK has decreased.

There are estimated to be only 140 000 red squirrels, and 2.5 million grey squirrels.

Calculate the percentage of squirrels in the UK that are red. Give your answer to one significant figure.

[2 marks]

_____ %

01.4 Grey squirrels eat the same food as the red squirrel but can also digest unripe acorns, while the red squirrel can only eat ripe acorns.

Explain why this is putting the red squirrel in danger of extinction. [2 marks]

_____

_____

_____

_____

01.5 Some scientists think that grey squirrels are also having a serious effect on the number of native woodland birds but red squirrels do not.

Suggest how scientists could collect data to test this hypothesis. [3 marks]

_____

_____

_____

_____

_____

_____

_____

02 Scientists have evidence of what the ancestors of some living organisms looked like.

02.1 Give one example of this evidence. [1 mark]

_____

02.2 Scientists think life began on Earth around 3 billion (3 000 000 000) years ago.

Write this number in standard form. [1 mark]

_____

02.3 Explain why scientists use standard form when talking about timescales involved in the history of the Earth. [2 marks]

_____

_____

_____

02.4 Explain why scientists cannot be certain how life on Earth began. [2 marks]

_____

_____

_____

_____

_____

_____

B15 Checklist

	Student Book	☺	☺	☹
I can describe the work of Gregor Mendel.	15.1			
I can explain how Mendel's work fits in with modern ideas of genetics.	15.1			
I can describe some theories of evolution.	15.2			
I can describe some of the evidence for evolution discovered by Darwin.	15.2			
I can explain why Darwin's theory of evolution was only gradually accepted.	15.3			
I can describe Wallace's ideas and explain how they influenced Darwin.	15.4			
I can describe how new species arise.	15.4			
I can explain the importance of isolation in speciation.	15.4			
I can give some evidence for the origins of life on Earth.	15.5			
I can describe how fossils are formed.	15.5			
I can describe what we can learn from fossils.	15.5			
I can explain what fossils can reveal about how organisms have changed over time.	15.6			
I can describe the ways that organisms can become extinct.	15.6			
I can describe how environmental change can cause extinction.	15.7			
I can describe how single catastrophic events can cause extinction on a massive scale.	15.7			
I can define antibiotic resistance.	15.8			
I can describe the part played by mutation in the development of antibiotic resistant strains of bacteria.	15.8			
I can describe how people can reduce the rate of development of antibiotic resistant strains such as MRSA.	15.8			
I can outline the basic principles of classification and the system developed by Linnaeus.	15.9			
I can use the binomial naming system of genus and species.	15.9			
I can describe how new technologies have changed classification.	15.9 15.10			
I can explain how scientists use evolutionary trees.	15.10			

B16.1 The importance of communities

A Fill in the gaps to complete the sentences.

The interaction of a community of living organisms with non-living (abiotic) parts is called an _____ .

Organisms require materials from their surroundings to survive. They need other living organisms to help

them reproduce, for _____, and for shelter. Plants require other organisms for pollination and

_____ dispersal.

If one species is removed it can affect the whole community. This is called _____ . A _____

community is one in which all the living organisms and abiotic parts are in balance so that population sizes remain

fairly constant.

B Give the terms being described:

a The populations of different species of living organisms living in a habitat _____

b The non-living factors in an environment _____

c The living factors in an environment _____

d Made up of different species of organisms interacting with the non-living factors of their environment

_____

C a Define the term 'stable community'.

_____

_____

b Give one example of a stable community. _____

D Within a community, the different animals and plants are often interdependent.

Describe the different ways that plants and animals are dependent on each other for survival.

_____

_____

_____

_____

B16.2 Organisms in their environment

A Fill in the gaps to complete the sentences.

Abiotic factors that may affect communities of organisms include: moisture levels, _____ intensity,

wind intensity and direction, soil pH and _____ content, temperature, the _____

_____ level in the air for plants, and the availability of oxygen for aquatic animals.

_____ factors that may affect communities of organisms include: availability of _____ , new

competitors, new predators arriving, and new pathogens.

B Factors that affect organisms in woodland can be living (biotic) or non-living (abiotic).

a Give **two** abiotic factors that will affect:

the **animals** living in the woodland.

1 _____

2 _____

the **plants** living in the woodland.

1 _____

2 _____

b Give **two** biotic factors that will affect **both** the animals and the plants:

1 _____

2 _____

C The diagram is part of a woodland food web.

There is an outbreak of a disease that kills only ladybirds.

Use the food web to explain how this affects the
population of other organisms in the woodland.

a The number of ladybirds

_____

_____

_____

_____

b The number of aphids

_____

_____

_____

_____

c The number of caterpillars

_____

_____

B16.3 Distribution and abundance

A Fill in the gaps to complete the sentences.

Scientists called _____ study the make-up of ecosystems. They look at how abiotic and

_____ factors affect organisms. They study the _____ of organisms (how common

they are) and their _____ (where they are). Ecologists also study the effect of changes in the environment

on the organisms in a particular ecosystem.

_____ are used to estimate the population of plants in an area. A line _____ can be used

to show how the distribution of organisms changes between two points.

B Scientists placed a line transect from the water's edge up to the top of a rocky shore.

They counted the number of barnacles and mussels found in a 0.25 m² area at different places along the transect. To do this they used the equipment shown opposite.

a What is this equipment called?

_____

b Show how the area of this equipment was calculated.

_____

C The scientists' results are shown below.

Distance from the water's edge in m	Number of mussels per 0.25 m²	Number of barnacles per 0.25 m²
0	0	0
5	6	0
10	18	0
15	12	9
20	7	16

Draw **two** conclusions from the data.

1 _____

_____

2 _____

_____

D Calculate an estimate for the number of barnacles per square metre living 15 m from the water's edge.

_____

B16.4 Competition in animals

A Fill in the gaps to complete the sentences.

Animals compete with each other for food, territories, and a _____ (an organism to breed with). The

best- _____ organisms are those most likely to win the competition for resources, so they will survive

and reproduce to produce healthy _____ .

There is competition between members of the same species and between members of _____ species.

B Give **three** things that animals compete for.

1 _____

2 _____

3 _____

C Foxes are omnivores. This means they eat a range of both plants and animals.

Using what you know about competition between animals, explain how this helps them to survive.

_____

_____

D Animal behaviours are often linked to competition for resources.

Explain the reason for each of the behaviours below:

a The peacock displays brightly coloured tail feathers.

_____

_____

b The male leopard scratches marks onto trees.

_____

_____

c A fox runs quickly when it sees a rabbit.

_____

_____

B16.5 Competition in plants

A Fill in the gaps to complete the sentences.

Plans _____ with each other for light for photosynthesis, to make _____ ; for

_____ for photosynthesis and for keeping their tissues rigid and supported; for nutrients (minerals) from

the _____ ; and for space to grow.

Plants have many _____ that make them good competitors.

B Plants compete with each other for resources.

For each resource they compete for, explain why it is important for healthy plant growth.

a Light

_____

b Space

_____

c Minerals from the soil

_____

d Water

_____

C For each of the adaptations below, explain how it helps the plant to avoid competition.

a Ivy has suckers that help it to grow up structures.

_____

_____

b The seeds of the maple tree are winged and flutter to the ground.

_____

_____

c The roots of the saguaro cactus spread far from the plant.

_____

_____

D A group of students carried out an investigation into the effect of competition on plants. Their results are shown opposite.

Give:

a The independent variable

_____

b The **two** dependent variables

1 _____

2 _____

c **Two** control variables they would have used

1 _____

2 _____

d A conclusion

_____

B16.6 Adapt and survive

A Fill in the gaps to complete the sentences.

Organisms, including microorganisms, have features (_____) that enable them to survive in

the conditions in which they normally live. _____ have adaptations that enable them to live

in environments with extreme conditions of salt concentration, _____ , or pressure.

B Different organisms require different resources to survive.

Give an explanation for the following statements:

a A cactus does not need oxygen.

_____

_____

b All organisms need water.

_____

_____

c An oak tree needs light, but a bacterial cell does not.

_____

_____

C Organisms that survive and reproduce in the most difficult conditions are known as extremophiles.

Use the description of their adaptations to suggest what kind of extreme condition each animal lives in.

a Has chemicals in cells that prevent ice crystals forming

_____

b Special cytoplasm in cells to stop water moving out by osmosis

_____

c Very large eyes and feelers

_____

D Microorganisms that live in conditions with high temperatures have specially adapted enzymes.

Describe how their enzymes are adapted.

Explain why this is important to their survival.

_____

_____

_____

B16.7 Adaptation in animals

A Fill in the gaps to complete the sentences.

Animals have adaptations that help them to get the resources they need to survive and reproduce. These include:

- _____ adaptations, for example camouflage or blubber for insulation

- behavioural adaptations, such as _____ to move to a better climate for the summer

- _____ adaptations related to processes such as reproduction and metabolism, for example, antifreeze in the cells of fish that live in cold water.

B Adaptations in animals can be structural, behavioural, or functional.

For each adaptation below, identify what type it is.

a Migration to warmer climate in the winter _____

b Thick fur for insulation _____

c Kidneys that can produce very concentrated urine _____

d Sleeping in cool burrows during the day _____

e Camouflaged fur _____

C The picture opposite shows a fennec fox. It lives in the Sahara desert, North Africa.

a Describe **one** structural adaptation that helps it to survive the hot days.

_____

_____

_____

b Describe **one** structural adaptation that helps it to survive the cold nights.

_____

D Emperor penguins live in Antarctica where the temperature can be as low as −30 °C.

a Fully grown penguins are large, growing up to around 1.2 m in height.

Explain how being large helps the penguin to survive.

_____

_____

_____

b When it is very cold, penguins huddle together.

Explain how this helps them to survive the conditions.

_____

_____

_____

B16.8 Adaptations in plants

A Fill in the gaps to complete the sentences.

Plants have adaptations that enable them to survive in the conditions in which they normally live.

Common plant adaptations include:

- for plants that live in hot conditions, a low surface area to volume ratio to _____ water loss from leaves

- protection from herbivores, for example the sharp _____ on a cactus

- extensive _____ systems, to collect as much water as possible in dry conditions

- storing _____ in tissues, to use in periods of dry weather.

B Cacti are plants that are adapted to live in hot, dry deserts.

For each of the adaptations below, explain how it helps the cactus to survive.

a Leaves are spines

_____

b Roots spread over a wide area

_____

c Stem stores water

_____

C Plants that live in very hot, dry conditions have a problem with water loss.

Marram grass has tightly curled leaves. The diagram shows a cross-section of a leaf.

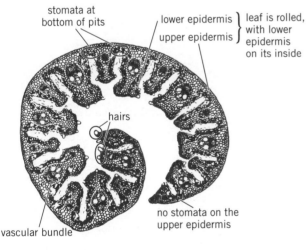

stomata at bottom of pits

lower epidermis
upper epidermis } leaf is rolled, with lower epidermis on its inside

hairs

no stomata on the upper epidermis

vascular bundle

Use it to explain how the leaves of the marram grass are adapted to reduce water loss.

_____

_____

_____

_____

_____

B16 Practice questions

01 **Figure 1** shows a water lily.

Water lilies are plants that grow in water. Their leaves and flowers float on the surface of the water.

Figure 1

01.1 On most plants stomata are located on the lower surface of the leaves.

In water lily leaves, the stomata are found on the upper surface (the surface that faces the air).

Explain an advantage of this adaptation.   [2 marks]

_____

_____

_____

01.2 A group of scientists studied the biomass of water lily plants growing in two different ponds, A and B.

They found that the biomass was higher in pond A compared to pond B.

Explain how abiotic (non-living) factors could cause this difference.   [4 marks]

_____

_____

_____

_____

_____

_____

02 A group of students were asked to estimate the number of dandelions on the school field. **Figure 2** shows the field.

Figure 2

02.1 Calculate the area of the field.   [2 marks]

_____ m²

02.2 They decided to sample areas of the field using a quadrat. They plan to place the quadrat in areas where there are many dandelions.

Explain why this is **not** a good idea.

Describe what they should do instead.   [3 marks]

_____

_____

_____

_____

02.3 The results from the investigation are shown in **Table 1**.

Table 1

Quadrat number	Number of dandelions
1	0
2	1
3	3
4	0
5	2
6	1
7	3
8	1
9	1
10	2

What is the mode of the number of dandelions counted?   [1 mark]

_____

02.4 Calculate the mean number of dandelions. Show your working out.   [2 marks]

_____

02.5 The area of the quadrat is 0.5m².

Carry out a calculation to estimate the number of dandelions in the field.

Show your working out.   [3 marks]

_____

B16 Checklist

	Student Book	☺	☺	☹
I can define the term stable community.	16.1			
I can describe how organisms are adapted to the conditions in which they live.	16.1			
I can explain the relationship between communities and ecosystems.	16.1			
I can name some of the factors that affect communities.	16.2			
I can describe how to measure the distribution of living things in their natural environment.	16.3			
I can calculate the mean, median, and mode of data.	16.3			
I can describe why animals compete.	16.4			
I can name the factors that animals are competing for in a habitat.	16.4			
I can describe how animals are adapted to the environment they live in.	16.4			
I can describe what makes an animal a successful competitor.	16.4			
I can identify what plants compete for.	16.5			
I can describe how plants compete.	16.5			
I can describe adaptations that plants have to make them successful competitors.	16.5			
I can describe what organisms need in order to survive.	16.6			
I can describe how organisms are adapted to survive in many different conditions.	16.6			
I can name some of the ways in which animals are adapted in order to survive.	16.7			
I can name some of the ways in which plants are adapted in order to survive.	16.8			

B17.1 Feeding relationships

A Fill in the gaps to complete the sentences.

Photosynthetic organisms (green plants and _____) are the producers of biomass.

Feeding relationships can be represented by food chains. All food chains begin with a _____ ,
which is eaten by primary _____ . These may be eaten by secondary consumers, which may be eaten
by _____ consumers.

Consumers that eat other animals (their prey) are _____ . In a stable community the numbers of
predators and prey rise and fall in cycles.

B The diagram shows part of a food web in the African savannah.

Use the food web to answer the following questions.

a Name **one** producer. _____

b Name **two** primary consumers. _____

and _____

c Name **three** predators.

1 _____

2 _____

3 _____

d Draw an example of a food chain that contains **four** organisms.

_____

_____

lion

cheetah   leopard

giraffe   impala   zebra

acacia tree   grass

C A population of rabbits lives in a field. Foxes are predators of rabbits.

Study the graph.

a Label the lines to show which represents the population of
foxes and which represents the population of rabbits.

b Describe how the population of both animals changes.

_____

_____

_____

_____

population size

time

c Explain the reason for this pattern.

_____

_____

_____

_____

_____

B17.2 Materials cycling

A Fill in the gaps to complete the sentences.

Materials such as water and carbon are constantly recycled to provide resources for organisms. The

_____ of dead animals and plants by microorganisms returns mineral ions to the _____ .

The water _____ describes how fresh water is available for plants and animals on land before draining

into the seas. Water is continuously evaporated, condensed, and _____ as rain or snow.

B The mineral ions in a cow's muscles were once part of a bird.

Describe the steps that took place to enable this recycling process.

_____

_____

_____

_____

C Explain the role of decomposers in ecosystems.

_____

_____

_____

_____

D Label the diagram, using the stages of the water cycle.

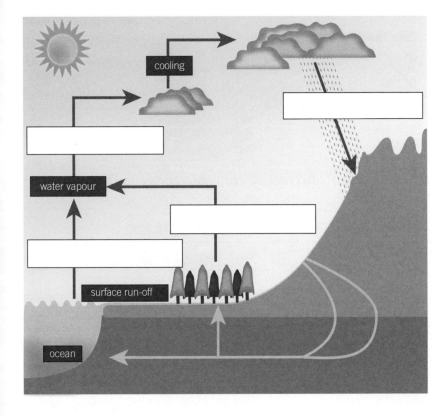

cooling

water vapour

surface run-off

ocean

B17.3 The carbon cycle

A Fill in the gaps to complete the sentences.

Carbon is recycled by the carbon _____ . The burning of fossil _____ , respiration,

and the _____ of dead plants and animals by microorganisms return carbon to the atmosphere as

_____ _____ . Plants take up carbon dioxide during _____ . The carbon is

stored in their tissues. The carbon is passed to animals when they _____ plants.

B For each statement below, write down the process it is describing:

a glucose + oxygen → carbon dioxide + water _____

b How carbon is passed from plants to animals _____

c The process that takes place in plants and removes carbon dioxide from the air _____

d The burning of fuels, which releases carbon dioxide into the air _____

C Write the processes from activity **B** on the diagram below to complete the carbon cycle.

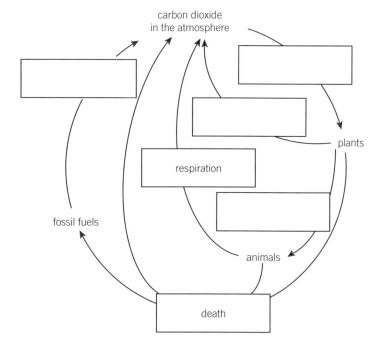

D The amount of carbon dioxide in the atmosphere remained fairly constant for millions of years.

Using the carbon cycle, explain why.

_____

_____

_____

_____

B17.4 Rates of decomposition

A Fill in the gaps to complete the sentences.

Factors that affect the rate of decay of organic matter are temperature, the availability of _____ gas and

_____ levels.

Gardeners and farmers try to provide _____ conditions for the rapid decay of waste organic matter.

The _____ produced is used as a natural fertiliser.

_____ decay produces methane gas. Biogas generators are used to produce methane gas so it can be

used as a _____

B The rate of decay is affected by temperature.

On the graph axes below, draw a line to show the relationship between the variables.

C A gardener buys a new compost maker.

a Explain why the gardener wants to make compost.

_____

b Explain how following each of these instructions helps increase how fast the compost is produced.

Place the compost maker in a place that receives plenty of sunlight.

_____

_____

Add water to the compost regularly so it does not dry out.

_____

_____

Occasionally, mix the contents.

_____

_____

D The diagram shows a biogas generator.

It produces methane, which is used as a fuel.

Suggest why:

a the generator is placed in the ground.

_____

_____

b the narrow opening is sealed after waste is added.

_____

_____

B17 Practice questions

01 When milk decays, microorganisms convert lactose in milk into lactic acid.

A group of students used a **model** to investigate how temperature affects the rate of decay of milk.

In the model, lipase is added to the milk. Fatty acids are formed.

This is the method they followed:

1 Add 5 drops of phenolphthalein to a test tube.

2 Add 5 cm³ of milk and 7 cm³ of sodium carbonate solution to the test tube. The solution should be pink.

4 Place the test tube in a water bath set at 40 °C and leave until the contents reach the same temperature.

5 Add 1 cm³ of lipase and start the stop-clock.

6 Stir the contents of the test tube until the solution loses its pink colour. Record the time.

7 Repeat for temperatures of 10 °C, 20 °C, and 30 °C.

01.1 Phenolphthalein is an indicator. It is pink in alkaline conditions and goes colourless in acidic conditions.

Describe why it is used in this investigation.

[2 marks]

_____

_____

01.2 Give **one** advantage and **one** disadvantage to using this model to investigate how temperature affects the rate of decay of milk. [2 marks]

Advantage _____

_____

Disadvantage _____

_____

01.3 Write a prediction for this investigation.

You should include a scientific reason for your prediction. [3 marks]

_____

_____

_____

_____

02 When plants die, they may decompose.

02.1 Define the term **decompose.** [2 marks]

_____

_____

_____

_____

02.2 In wet areas, such as marshes, plants decompose at a slow rate.

Suggest why plants decompose slowly in marshes.

[2 marks]

_____

_____

02.3 The dead plant material in the soil is called humus and is used as food by earthworms.

The worms are eaten by birds called thrushes. Thrushes are eaten by hawks.

Use this information to draw the food chain in the space below. [2 marks]

B17 Checklist

	Student Book	☺	☺	☹
I can describe the importance of photosynthesis in feeding relationships.	17.1			
I can describe the main feeding relationships within a community.	17.1			
I can explain how the numbers of predators and prey in a community are related.	17.1			
I can describe how materials are recycled in a stable community.	17.2			
I can explain the importance of decay.	17.2			
I can describe what the carbon cycle is.	17.3			
I can describe the processes that remove carbon dioxide from the atmosphere and return it again.	17.3			
I can describe what affects the rate of decay.	17.4			
I can describe how to make compost.	17.4			

B18.1 The human population explosion

A Fill in the gaps to complete the sentences.

_____ is the variety of all the different species of organisms on Earth, or within an ecosystem.

Humans reduce the amount of land available for other animals and plants by building, quarrying, farming, and

dumping _____ .

The future of the human species on Earth relies on us maintaining a _____ level of biodiversity. Many

human activities are _____ biodiversity.

The human population is _____ rapidly. This means that more _____ are being used and

more waste is produced.

B A forest has high biodiversity.

Describe what this means.

_____

C Human activity can affect biodiversity.

For each activity, describe how it affects the biodiversity of the area.

a Cutting down a natural tropical rainforest to form an oil palm plantation

_____

_____

b Using chemical pesticides on farmland

_____

_____

D The graph opposite shows recorded and predicted human populations.

a Give the human population in 1960.

_____

b Describe how the graph predicts human population will change.

_____

_____

c Explain why these predictions may not be accurate.

_____

_____

B18.2 Land and water pollution

A Fill in the gaps to complete the sentences.

If waste is not handled properly it may pollute the land and water. Pollution can occur on land from landfill

and from toxic _____ such as pesticides and herbicides. These may also be washed from land to

_____ .

Pollution can occur in water from sewage, _____ (which are used to increase plant growth), or

toxic chemicals. Pollution kills plants and animals, which can _____ biodiversity.

B The graph shows how some abiotic factors change along a river.

Some nuclear power plants take cold water from a river and use it to cool down their reactors.

The resulting warmed water is released back into the river.

a A nuclear power plant is located along the river.

Use the graph to suggest the distance down river it is located. _____

b Use the graph to predict how the biodiversity of living organisms will be affected at this location.

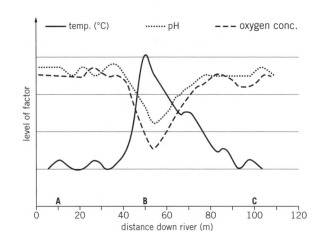

_____

_____

_____

C Fertilisers are added to the soil on farms to increase crop yields. The fertilisers can run into nearby lakes. Explain why this can lead to a reduction in biodiversity in a lake.

_____

_____

_____

_____

D A group of scientists measured the pH, oxygen, and nitrate levels in three different lakes. Their data is shown below.

Which lake is each statement describing?

Write the letter of the lake in the space. Give a reason for your answer.

a can support a high level of biodiversity

_____

Lake	pH	Oxygen level	Nitrate level
X	6.5	normal	normal
Y	7.2	high	low
Z	7.9	low	high

_____

b is polluted with fertilisers _____

_____

c is most likely to have the lowest level of biodiversity _____

_____

B18.3 Air pollution

A Fill in the gaps to complete the sentences.

Pollution can occur in the _____ from smoke and from acidic gases. When fossil _____

are burnt, acidic gases are formed that dissolve in rainwater to form acid _____ . Acid rain damages the

environment. It can kill trees and make lakes and streams acidic.

Smoke pollution causes an increase in tiny particulates in the air, which can cause global _____ and

affect human health.

B Name the following:

a The haze of smoke particles and acidic gases that is common in some cities.

_____

b The tiny solid particles found in smoke.

_____

c Fuels, including coal and oil, that release acidic gases when burnt.

_____

C The graph shows sulfur dioxide emissions in four different countries between 1850 and 2005.

a Describe the overall trend in sulfur dioxide emissions between 1975 and 2005 for:

China _____

The UK _____

b Suggest reasons for the trends.

China _____

_____

The UK _____

_____

c Describe the effects of sulfur dioxide pollution on living organisms.

_____

_____

_____

_____

_____

_____

_____

B18.4 Deforestation and peat destruction

A Fill in the gaps to complete the sentences.

Deforestation is the removal of _____ without replacing them. Large-scale deforestation is used to provide land for farming and to grow crops for biofuels.

Peat is made of plant material that has not completely _____ . The destruction of peat bogs to produce garden compost _____ biodiversity in this habitat. The decay or burning of peat releases _____ _____ into the atmosphere.

B Write down:

a **two** reasons why deforestation increases the amount of carbon dioxide in the atmosphere.

1 _____

2 _____

b **three** reasons why deforestation is being carried out.

1 _____

2 _____

3 _____

C In 1970 there were an estimated 4 100 000 km² of rainforest in Brazil.

In 2015 this area was estimated to be 3 331 065 km².

a Calculate the estimated area of forest lost in Brazil between 1970 and 2015.

_____ km²

b Calculate the percentage of forest lost during this time.

_____ %

D Sara is shopping for compost at a garden centre. She has to decide whether to buy peat or peat-free compost.

a Describe why peat is a useful compost.

_____

_____

b Explain the environmental benefits of using peat-free compost.

_____

_____

_____

c Suggest **one** other factor that could affect her decision.

_____

B18.5 Global warming

A Fill in the gaps to complete the sentences.

Because of human activity, levels of carbon dioxide and _____ in the atmosphere are increasing.

This is contributing to global _____ .

Consequences of global warming include:

- loss of habitat when low-lying areas are flooded by rising _____ levels

- changes in the distribution of species in areas where temperature or rainfall has changed

- changes to the _____ patterns of animals.

B Since the 1950s the amount of carbon dioxide in the atmosphere has been measured in Hawaii.

The graph opposite shows the data.

a Describe the trend in the data.

_____

_____

b Suggest **one** reason for this trend.

_____

_____

_____

Atmospheric CO_2 at Mauna Loa observatory

C Explain why an increase in the emissions of greenhouse gases is linked to global warming.

_____

_____

_____

D The biodiversity of insects in the UK is expected to change because of climate change.

Suggest one reason why:

a Biodiversity may increase.

_____

_____

b Biodiversity may decrease.

_____

_____

B18.6 The impact of change

A Fill in the gaps to complete the sentences.

Environmental changes such as availability of _____, temperature, and atmospheric gases affect the

_____ of species in an ecosystem.

These changes may be seasonal, geographic, or caused by _____ interaction.

B An ecologist used a line transect to show the distribution of plant species of some sand dunes.

Suggest **three** environmental factors that could influence this change in distribution.

1 _____

2 _____

3 _____

C The round-leaved sundew is a plant that grows on peat bogs.

The acidic soils in these habitats do not supply the plant with enough nutrients so it has adapted to be a carnivorous plant, digesting insects that become trapped on its sticky leaves.

a Explain why the round-leaved sundew is only found in some areas of the UK.

_____

_____

b Suggest how human interaction is changing the distribution of the plant.

_____

_____

D Many birds, such as the ringed plover, migrate from northern Europe to warmer climates during the winter.

Suggest how climate change is affecting the distribution of populations of these birds in the winter.

_____

_____

_____

_____

B18.7 Maintaining biodiversity

A Fill in the gaps to complete the sentences.

Scientists and concerned citizens have put programmes in place to reduce the negative effects of humans on ecosystems and biodiversity.

These include _____ programmes for endangered species, protection and regeneration of rare

habitats, the reintroduction of field margins and _____ , the reduction of deforestation, and

recycling _____ .

B Many zoos carry out breeding programmes.

There are benefits and drawbacks of breeding programmes in zoos.

a Describe **one** benefit.

_____

_____

b Describe **one** drawback.

_____

_____

C Read the information below about landfill sites.

> Both household and industrial waste is taken to landfill sites to be buried in the ground.
>
> To build landfill sites large areas of land have to be cleared. This could be waste-ground or it could be land that is the habitat to many plants and animals.
>
> When the rubbish is in the ground some chemicals can leak out of the rubbish and enter the land or waterways.
>
> When the landfill site is full of rubbish, they can be covered in soil and planted with trees and bushes.

a Outline the environmental impacts of landfill sites.

_____

_____

_____

_____

b Suggest how people can reduce the amount of rubbish that goes to landfills.

_____

D Study the data in the chart opposite.

Describe what the chart shows.

_____

_____

_____

_____

_____

_____

Chart legend: total landfill; landfill tax. Y-axis left: million tonnes (0–9). Y-axis right: £ per tonne (0–60). X-axis: 2004 2005 2006 2007 2008 2009 2010.

B18.8 Trophic levels and biomass

A Fill in the gaps to complete the sentences.

_____ levels can be represented by numbers, starting at level 1. Level 1 organisms are the

_____ . Further trophic levels are numbered subsequently according to how far the organism is along

the food _____ .

_____ of biomass can be constructed to represent the relative amount of biomass at each level of a

food chain.

B Biomass is the mass of material in living organisms.

Explain how biomass is passed along a food chain.

_____

C The diagram shows a pyramid of biomass.

a Describe how the biomass of the organisms in each trophic level can be measured accurately.

_____

b Give a limitation of this method.

_____

c Describe how the amount of biomass changes at each trophic level.

_____

biomass of
tertiary consumer
(carnivore)

biomass of secondary
consumer (carnivore)

biomass of primary consumer
(herbivore)

biomass of producer
(plant or algae)

D A food chain from the ocean is:

phytoplankton → small fish → cormorants

Use the information from the table to draw a pyramid of biomass
for this food chain. Make sure the bars are drawn to scale and
labelled.

Trophic level	Dry biomass in kg
1	6000
2	600
3	60

B18.9 Biomass transfers

A Fill in the gaps to complete the sentences.

Producers are mostly plants and _____ that transfer about 1% of the incident energy from

_____ for photosynthesis.

Only approximately _____ % of the biomass from each trophic level is transferred to the level above it. This is

because biomass is lost from each level in faeces, in waste, and in the process of _____ to transfer

_____ for organisms.

B A food chain from a habitat is:

grass → rabbit → hawk

Only approximately 10% of the biomass from the rabbit is transferred to the hawk.

a Explain how the plant produces biomass.

_____

_____

b A rabbit has a biomass of 500 g.

Calculate the biomass transferred to a hawk when it eats the rabbit.

_____

C The table below gives information about what happens to the biomass eaten by a cow and a trout (a fish).

Organism	Percentage of biomass in food that can be used by the organism	Percentage of biomass in food that is used for respiration	Percentage of biomass in food that is used for growth
Cow	37.5	89.1	10.9
Trout	86.0	65.0	35.0

a Suggest why the percentage of biomass in food that is used by the organism is lower for the cow than the trout.

_____

_____

b Suggest why the cow uses more biomass for respiration than the trout.

_____

_____

c Give the name of the organism that will grow fastest. Give a reason for your answer.

_____

_____

D Explain how biomass from other organisms is passed to decomposers.

_____

_____

B18.10 Factors affecting food security

A Fill in the gaps to complete the sentences.

It is important for world health that everyone eats a _____ diet, to avoid all the diseases linked to eating too little, too much, or the wrong things.

Factors affecting food security include: increasing _____ rates; changing diets in developed countries;

new _____ and pathogens; environmental changes affecting food production; the cost of agricultural

inputs; and _____ affecting access to water or food.

B **a** Define the terms:

Food security

_____

Malnutrition

_____

Sustainable food production

_____

b Write a sentence linking these three terms.

_____

_____

C Explain how global warming has a negative impact on food security.

_____

_____

D The bar graph shows the relationship between birth rate and death rate for two countries.

Name the country that is at a higher risk of reduced food security.

Give a reason for your answer.

_____

_____

_____

_____

B18.11 Making food production efficient

A Fill in the gaps to complete the sentences.

The efficiency of food production can be improved by restricting _____ transfer from food animals

to the _____. This can be done by limiting their _____ and by controlling the

_____ of their surroundings.

Some animals are fed high _____ foods to increase growth.

B Explain why food security would increase if people ate less meat.

_____

_____

_____

_____

_____

C Chickens farmed for meat are sometimes kept inside in poultry rearing sheds. The chickens are ready to eat in a few weeks.

a Explain why each of these factors increases the growth of the chickens:

Controlling their movement

_____

_____

Controlling the temperature of the shed

_____

_____

b Give one economic advantage and one disadvantage to farming chickens in this way.

Advantage _____

_____

Disadvantage _____

_____

c Give one ethical argument against farming in this way.

_____

D Fish are a good source of protein.

They can be caught from the wild or farmed.

Compare the advantages of farming fish compared with fishing wild fish.

_____

_____

_____

_____

_____

_____

B18.12 Sustainable food production

A Fill in the gaps to complete the sentences.

It is important to maintain _____ stocks in our seas at a level where breeding continues or certain species may disappear altogether.

Modern _____ techniques enable large quantities of microorganisms to be cultured for food.

The _____ called *Fusarium* is useful for producing _____, a food rich in protein.

B Use the graph to answer the questions below.

a Describe the general trend in North Sea cod stocks between 1963 and 1999.

Give a reason for this trend.

_____

_____

_____

_____

b Suggest what has happened to North Sea cod stocks between 1999 and now.

Explain how you used the graph to decide your answer.

_____

_____

C In recent years, restrictions have been put in place on fishing in order to conserve fish populations.

a Describe **one** of these restrictions.

Explain how it helps to conserve fish populations.

_____

_____

_____

b Explain why people working in the fishing industry may be against these restrictions.

_____

_____

D The fungus *Fusarium* is a source of protein. It is grown inside fermenters.

One is shown in the diagram.

a Describe the function of each item:

Glucose syrup _____

pH probe _____

Oxygen _____

b Explain why *Fusarium* is a sustainable food source.

_____

_____

B18 Practice questions

01 Burning fossil fuels releases polluting gases into the atmosphere.

For each environmental effect, name a polluting gas that causes it. [2 marks]

Acid rain _____

Global warming _____

02 The graphs in **Figure 1** were published by the IPCC (Intergovernmental Panel on Climate Change).

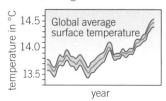 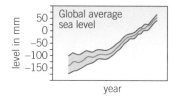

Figure 1

02.1 Describe the correlation between global average surface temperature and sea level. [1 mark]

HINT A correlation is a relationship: there is a link between the variables.

_____

_____

02.2 Suggest **one** explanation for this relationship. [2 marks]

_____

_____

02.3 Explain how this change in sea level could affect biodiversity. [3 marks]

_____

_____

_____

_____

_____

03 A group of students was asked to carry out an investigation into the effects of acid rain on living organisms.

They chose to investigate the hypothesis 'The more concentrated the acid rain, the fewer seeds will germinate.'

They used the following method.

1. Line five Petri dishes with cotton wool.
2. Place three cress seeds in each dish.

3. Every day, add water or sulfuric acid to the dishes. Use a different solution in each dish:
   - distilled water (0 g/dm³ sulfuric acid)
   - 10 g/dm³ sulfuric acid
   - 25 g/dm³ sulfuric acid
   - 50 g/dm³ sulfuric acid
   - 100 g/dm³ sulfuric acid.

4. After a week, count how many seeds have germinated. Calculate this as a percentage.

03.1 Describe how the method could be improved to produce more valid results. [4 marks]

_____

_____

_____

_____

_____

_____

03.2 After improving their method, the students carried out the investigation. **Table 1** shows their results.

Table 1

Concentration of sulfuric acid in g/dm³	Percentage of seeds that had germinated
0	92%
10	87%
25	62%
50	30%
100	5%

Plot these data as a line graph. [3 marks]

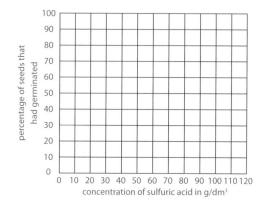

03.3 Explain if the data supports their hypothesis or not. [2 marks]

_____

_____

_____

B18 Checklist

	Student Book	☺	☺	☹
I can define biodiversity and explain why it is important.	18.1			
I can describe some of the effects of the growth in human population on the Earth and its resources.	18.1			
I can describe how human activities pollute the land.	18.2			
I can describe how human activities pollute the water.	18.2			
I can describe how acid rain is formed.	18.3			
I can explain how acid rain affects living organisms.	18.3			
I can describe how air pollution causes global dimming and smog.	18.3			
I can define deforestation.	18.4			
I can explain why loss of biodiversity matters.	18.4			
I can describe the environmental effects of destroying peat bogs.	18.4			
I can define global warming.	18.5			
I can explain how global warming could affect life on Earth.	18.5			
I can evaluate the effect of environmental changes on the distribution of organisms.	18.6			
I can name the different types of environmental changes.	18.6			
I can describe how waste, deforestation, and global warming all have an impact on biodiversity.	18.7			
I can describe some of the ways people are trying to reduce the impact of human activities on ecosystems and maintain biodiversity.	18.7			
I can describe what a trophic level is.	18.8			
I can construct accurate pyramids of biomass from appropriate data.	18.8			
I can explain how biomass is lost by organisms at each stage of a food chain.	18.9			
I can describe some of the factors that threaten global food security.	18.10			
I can explain why short food chains make food production more efficient.	18.11			
I can describe how farmers manage food production to reduce wasted energy and therefore loss of biomass.	18.11			
I can evaluate the advantages and disadvantages of modern farming techniques.	18.11			
I can define sustainable food production.	18.12			
I can describe how to conserve fish stocks and make fishing for food sustainable again.	18.12			
I can describe how fungi can be used to make a sustainable protein source.	18.12			

Answers

B1.1

A magnify, small, electrons, magnification, resolution / resolving power, larger / bigger, more

B slide – **Y**   objective lens – **X**
eyepiece lens – **W**   light – **Z**

C $\dfrac{15}{100\,000} = 0.000\,15\,mm$
$0.000\,15 \times 1000 = \textbf{0.15}\,\mu m$

D light; because it is cheaper, smaller, and easier to use than an electron microscope; it will have a high enough resolving power and magnification to carry out the task

B1.2

A nucleus, cytoplasm, membrane, energy, proteins, wall, chloroplasts, vacuole

B **a** contains genes that carry the instructions for making proteins
b controls the passage of substances into and out of the cell
c where proteins are made
d where aerobic respiration takes place, which releases energy
e where most of the chemical reactions in the cell take place

C cell membrane, ribosomes, mitochondria, cytoplasm, nucleus

D found only in plants – chloroplast, cell wall, permanent vacuole; found in both animals and plants – nucleus, mitochondria, cell membrane

B1.3

A eukaryotic, nucleus, prokaryotic, nucleus, plasmids

B similarities: both have a cell membrane, cytoplasm, ribosomes, mitochondria, genetic material, cell wall (in common with plant and fungal cells); differences: a prokaryotic cell wall does not contain cellulose (like a plant cell), prokaryotes do not have a nucleus (their genetic material exists as a single chromosome plus plasmids)

C **a** for movement
b contain extra genes such as those for antibiotic resistance
c for protection

D **a** $\dfrac{100}{1000} = 0.1\,mm$
b $\dfrac{1}{1000} = 0.001\,m$
c $\dfrac{1}{0.1} = 10 = 1$ order of magnitude

B1.4

A differentiate, specialised, function, nerve, muscle, egg

B **a** muscle cell   **b** egg cell
c nerve cell / neurone

C nucleus which contains half the genetic information from the father; streamlined shape to help it move quickly; tail / flagella for movement to egg to fertilise it; extra mitochondria to provide energy for movement of tail; enzymes in the head to break down the outer layer of the egg so sperm nucleus can fuse with egg nucleus during fertilisation

D answer names a place in the human body where ciliated cells are found, e.g. lungs / trachea / small intestine / fallopian tubes (oviducts); and explains their function in this place, e.g. the cilia move mucus that has trapped particles away from the lungs / the cilia help move egg along fallopian tube to the uterus

B1.5

A specialised, area, water, lignin, sieve
B photosynthetic / leaf / palisade cell, xylem cell, phloem cell
C **a** phloem   **b** xylem
c strengthens the xylem so it can withstand the water pressure and helps support the plant stem
D **a** root hair cell
b has projection / 'hair'; this increases surface area to increase uptake of water (and mineral ions)

B1.6

A movement, higher, lower, rate, gradient, area, oxygen
B **B** should show partial mixing of the particles

C should show particles equally distributed
C **two** from: larger surface area of leaf; higher temperature; higher concentration of carbon dioxide outside of leaf; lower concentration of carbon dioxide inside leaf
D it has small protections (microvilli) that increase the surface area of the cell

B1.7

A diffusion, water, concentrated, membrane, water, same, hypertonic, hypotonic
B **a** arrow going from left to right
b the net movement of water during osmosis is from a higher water concentration (lower solute concentration) to a lower water concentration (higher solute concentration)
C hypotonic, hypertonic, isotonic
D **X** – the cell would swell up and burst; **Y** – the cell would become shrivelled
E it prevents too much water entering or leaving cells by osmosis; if the solute concentration in the blood plasma increases, then water concentration will decrease and water will leave surrounding cells; the cells will become shrivelled; if the solute concentration in the blood plasma decreases, then water concentration will increase and water will enter surrounding cells; the cells will burst; damage to cells is harmful to the organism

B1.8

A turgor, loses, flaccid, membrane, plasmolysis
B **a** the solution surrounding the plant cells is less concentrated than the cell contents (hypotonic), water moves into the cell by osmosis; this causes the vacuole to swell, which presses the cytoplasm against the plant cell wall causing pressure
b the solution surrounding the plant cells is more concentrated than the cell contents (hypertonic), water will leave the cells by osmosis
c more water is lost by osmosis, the vacuole and cytoplasm shrink, and the cell membrane pulls away from the cell wall
C **a** curved line of best fit drawn
b point at (80, −20) is circled
c **i** mass of potato discs **increased** because there was a net movement of water **into** the potato cells by osmosis; concentration of water in potato cells was lower than in the surrounding solution
ii mass of potato discs **did not change** because there was **no** net movement of water; concentration of water in potato cells and the surrounding solution was the same
iii mass of potato discs **decreased** because there was a net movement of water **out of** the potato cells by osmosis; concentration of water in potato cells was higher than in the surrounding solution

B1.9

A dilute, gradient, respiration, root, soil, higher
B **a** they are both a process used to move substances across a cell membrane
b **one** from: active transport is an active process, it needs energy to take place; diffusion is a passive process, it does not require any energy; active transport moves substances from a low to high concentration (against the concentration gradient); diffusion moves substances from a high to low concentration (along the concentration gradient)
C **a** as the rate of respiration increases, so does the rate of active transport
b if the roots do not have access to enough oxygen, they cannot carry out respiration to release energy and so active transport of mineral ions from the soil into the roots cannot take place; the plant cannot manufacture proteins and so will die

B1.10

A large, decreases, large, thin, blood, fish

B X – 2 – 4 – **24** – 8 – 3:1
Y – 4 – **16** – 96 – **64** – 1.5:1

C unicellular organisms can use diffusion to supply all parts of the cell with substances and release waste products into their surroundings; multicellular organisms are made up of many cells so cannot use diffusion alone to supply them with substances and remove waste; they need a circulatory system to transport these substances to and from cells

D two from: large surface area; good blood supply; thin walls

B1 Practice questions

01.1 chloroplasts; [1] carry out photosynthesis [1]

01.2 10 × 1000 = 10 000 [1]

$\frac{10}{10\,000}$ = 1000 [1] = 3 (orders of magnitude) [1]

02.1 osmosis [1]

02.2 cut up plant tissue, e.g. potato, into pieces of a similar mass and shape; [1] measure the mass of each one using balances / scales; [1] submerge each in a different concentration of sugar solution; [1] leave for a specified time, e.g. 30 minutes; [1] remove plant tissue and dry; [1] measure the mass and calculate mass change [1]

03 three from: tail to move through the female reproductive system to the egg; [1] mitochondria to supply energy (to the tail); [1] enzymes to break down the outer layers of the egg; [1] genes / genetic information from the father; [1] streamlined shape to help it move quickly [1]

B2.1

A cycle, two, mitosis, repair

B **a** a molecule that contains the genetic code of an organism

b a small piece of DNA that controls a characteristic, or part of a characteristic

c a string of genes

d part of the cell where genetic material is found

C **a** there is one from each parent

b middle cell – 20; bottom cells – 10

D during stage 1 of the cell cycle the DNA replicates; during stage 2 (mitosis) the nucleus divides; during stage 3 the cell splits into two

B2.2

A differentiate, embryos, meristems, root

B differentiation is the process by which stem cells (unspecialised cells) become specialised; it is important because organisms need specialised cells to carry out different functions in the body

C **a** two from: differentiation occurs when stem cells turn into specialised cells; differentiation is permanent (specialised cells cannot turn back into stem cells); differentiation happens throughout life

b in animals, stem cells are found in several different places, in plants they are only found in regions called meristems; in animals, most types of differentiation only occurs in early life (not in adults), in plants differentiation can happen throughout life

D the tips of roots and shoots in regions called meristems

B2.3

A adult, diabetes, meristems, quickly

B **a** e.g., paralysis; type 1 diabetes

b adult, embryonic

c **three** from: brain, blood, bone marrow, liver, muscle

C **a** it is a meristem region so contains stem cells, which can develop into a whole new plant

b the powder promotes the growth of roots, so the plant can take up water that it needs to photosynthesise and grow

c the bag stops the plant losing too much water, as at first its roots will not be developed enough to take up enough water

B2.4

A risks, ethical, therapeutic, reject, adult

B X, Z, W, V, Y

C answer should include: **the possible benefit of stem cell research** – the possibility of using stem cells to treat conditions such as paralysis and diabetes; these diseases are currently incurable; the treatment has to have the potential to improve many lives; **a possible risk** – embryonic stem cells might cause cancer if they are used to treat people; more research needs to be done to make sure it is safe; **an ethical concern** – the embryos will be destroyed after being used; some people feel that this is not right because embryos have the potential to become a person and so have a right to life; **an economic concern**: the research is expensive and some people feel that the money spent would be better spent on research into other areas of medicine; **a justified conclusion**: e.g., I think stem cell research should be used because the possible benefits outweigh the concerns

B2 Practice questions

01.1 therapeutic cloning [1]

01.2 **one** from: paralysis; [1] type 1 diabetes; [1] any other sensible answer, e.g. any inherited illness [1]

01.3 **two** from: can differentiate into any cell; [1] will not be rejected by the patient; [1] divide and grow rapidly [1]

01.4 the embryo is a potential new life / has a right to life; [1] once the cells are removed, the embryo is destroyed [1]

02.1 **one** from: to produce new cells for growth; [1] to replace worn out skin cells; [1] to produce offspring in asexual reproduction [1]

02.2 stage 2 (mitosis), stage 1, stage 3 [1]

02.3 48 × 2 = 96 [1]

02.4 $\frac{20}{360}$ × 37 [1] = 2 (hours) [1]

03 stem and roots contain meristem tissue; this contains unspecialised cells; [1] these can differentiate to form different tissues and a new plant; [1] most animal cells differentiate permanently early in embryo development; [1] the cells cannot change back to being unspecialised [1]

B3.1

A cells, muscle, tissues, stomach, glandular, systems, digestive

B cells of the same type are grouped to form tissues; different tissues are arranged to form organs, each tissue has a different function in the organ; organs are grouped to form organ systems, which carry out life processes in the organism

C muscular, epithelial, glandular

D **a** **i** circulatory **ii** excretory
iii gas exchange / respiratory

b to break down large, insoluble food molecules into smaller soluble molecules that can diffuse into the bloodstream

B3.2

A digestive, organs, insoluble, small, bloodstream

B clockwise from top: gullet / oesophagus, stomach, large intestine, small intestine, liver

C **a** salivary, stomach, pancreas

b it produces protease enzyme, which helps to breakdown protein; it produces acid, which kills any microorganisms present in the food; it churns / squeezes the food to help mix it with protease and acid

c long so food stays in the small intestine for enough time for it to come into contact with enzymes so the food can be completely broken down into soluble substances; good blood supply so soluble food molecules can move into the blood so they can be transported around the body; large surface area to increase the efficiency of absorption of food molecules into the blood

B3.3

A proteins, starch / glycogen / cellulose, glycerol, amino

B carbohydrates – pasta / rice / bread / sugary food – provide energy – simple sugars (glucose)
lipids – butter / olive oil / nuts / avocado – provide energy, building new cell membranes and hormones – glycerol and fatty acids

proteins – meat / fish / nuts / dairy products / pulses – forming new tissues, enzymes, and hormones – amino acids

C **a** the hormone is the correct shape to fit into the receptor; it has to be the correct shape to trigger the response in the cell

  b if the pH changes the bonds holding the shape of the protein chain of the receptor will be broken; the receptor will change shape (denature); the hormone will no longer fit into the receptor

D **test for starch** – add iodine to the dry soup; if starch is present it will go a blue-black colour
test for protein – add some of the soup to water and mix well; add Biuret solution and leave; if protein is present then a purple colour will be present
test for glucose – add some of the soup to water and mix well; add Benedict's solution and place in a water bath; if glucose is present then a brick-red colour will be present

B3.4

A catalysts, rate, amino, active, substrate, key, metabolism, small, breaking

B a substance that increases the rate of a chemical reaction

C step 1: the **substrate** fits into the **active site** of the **enzyme**; step 2: the substrate breaks down to form the **products**; step 3: the products leave the active site and the enzyme is used again

D add a catalyst to the hydrogen peroxide and measure the volume of gas (oxygen) produced in one minute; repeat this three times; change the catalyst and repeat; compare the mean volume of gas produced; the catalyst that produced the most broke down the hydrogen peroxide at the fastest rate; control variables to use include the mass of catalyst, volume of hydrogen peroxide, temperature of hydrogen peroxide, room temperature

B3.5

A temperature, optimum, denature, active, substrate

B **a** place the test tube in a water bath; time how long it takes for the mixture to go clear; use a range of water bath temperatures, e.g. 0–50 °C

  b concentration of the albumin mixture / mass of albumin in 100 cm³ of water; pH of the mixture

  c **i** **trend** – as the temperature increases so does the rate of reaction; **explanation** – as the temperature increases the kinetic energy of the substrate and enzymes increase; there are more successful collisions between enzyme and substrate so more product is made within a time period

    ii **trend** – as the temperature increases the rate of reaction stays constant; **explanation** – this is the optimum temperature for the enzyme; all enzymes are working as quickly as

possible (as products leave, another substrate enters the active site)

    iii **trend** – as the temperature increases the rate of reaction decreases; **explanation** – as the temperature increases enzymes will start to denature (the active site will change shape so the substrate no longer fits); the higher the temperature, the more enzymes will be denatured; at 54 °C there are no working enzymes so the reaction stops

B3.6

A glands, insoluble, enzymes, protein, lipases, lipids

B amylase – **starch** – 1. mouth (salivary glands); 2. **pancreas**
protease – protein – 1. **stomach**; 2. pancreas; 3. **small intestine**
lipase – **lipids** – 1. **pancreas**; 2. small intestine

C **a** step 2

  b the pH of the mixture that resulted in the iodine colour change in the shortest amount of time is the optimum

  c the amylase was not breaking down the starch; this could be because: the amylase was not active as it was not warm enough / there was not enough amylase; to resolve this they can put the mixture in a water bath at 37 °C / use a higher concentration of amylase or a greater volume

D growth will be slowed down; enzymes to catalyse the breakdown of food molecules are prevented from reaching the food in the small intestine; less food is broken down; fewer nutrients in the bloodstream to aid growth, e.g. glucose used as an energy source and amino acids to build new tissue

B3.7

A acid, low, alkaline, liver, gall bladder, duct, neutralise, small

B bile is not an enzyme; a correct definition would be: 'bile emulsifies the fat into tiny droplets, which increases the surface area for lipase to increase the rate of digestion'

C bile neutralises the acidic liquid that comes from the stomach; so the liquid containing food in the small intestine is alkaline; this is the optimum pH for amylase; starch is broken down efficiently, releasing sugars

B3 Practice questions

01.1 clockwise from top: liver, pancreas, gall bladder [1 for all correct]

01.2 liver: produces bile; [1] gall bladder: stores bile and releases it into the small intestine [1]

02.1 $\frac{(91 + 88)}{2}$ [1] = 89.5 [1; only 1 mark in total if anomalous result of 139 is included in calculation]

02.2 the lipase was broken down into glycerol and fatty acids; [1] the pH of the mixture decreased / became acidic [1]

02.3 the phenolphthalein went colourless more quickly when bile was added to lipase

and oil; [1] bile increases the rate of oil breakdown; [1] bile emulsifies fat droplets to increase the surface area of the lipid; [1] so lipase works more efficiently [1]

02.4 get someone else to repeat the experiment using the same method; [1] compare the two sets of results [1]

B4.1

A heart, plasma, haemoglobin, lungs, (harmful) microorganisms / pathogens, clotting

B plasma; transport oxygen from the lungs to body cells; white blood cells; help the blood to clot at the site of a wound

C **one** risk from: risk of transfer of viruses, e.g. HIV, in the blood and causing disease in the patient; risk of immune response to the donor blood; **one** way of minimising the risk from: screen donor blood for viruses; use blood of the same blood group as the patient

D **a** the haemoglobin binds to oxygen in the lungs; when the red blood cells reach the body cells the oxygen is released

  b there is more room for cytoplasm, which contains haemoglobin

  c this gives them an increased surface area to volume ratio for diffusion of oxygen into and out of the cell

  d they can squeeze through narrow blood capillaries

B4.2

A veins, capillaries, valves, humans, double, lungs

B artery, vein, capillary

C **a** to pick up oxygen so it can be transported to respiring body cells

  b no, they have a single circulatory system; the blood only travels once through the heart on each circuit around the body

D **U**: capillaries; **V**: vein; **W**: artery; **X**: capillaries; **Y**: vein; **Z**: artery

B4.3

A blood, two, ventricle, lungs, left, valves, oxygen, stents, statins

B **a** pulmonary vein   **b** pulmonary artery
  c vena cava   **d** aorta

C blood enters the right and left atria; the atria contract; blood is pushed into the right and left ventricles; the ventricles contract; blood is pushed into the arteries and leaves the heart

D **a** stent; bypass surgery; statins

B4.4

A mechanical, animals, atrium, pacemaker, artificial, artificial

B **a** **both valves** – surgery is required to fit the valve, which is expensive; **mechanical valve** – they are expensive to make and the patient has to take drugs every day to stop clots forming; however, they last a long time before they need to be replaced; **biological valve** – they are cheap and the patient does not need to take drugs; however, they need to be replaced after 12–15 years which requires more expensive surgery

b some people may not choose to have a biological valve because it is from a living organism / a human / pig / cow and this goes against their beliefs

c the benefits are that the heart will work more efficiently, allowing the patient to have a better quality of life without the need for drugs; there is the risk of death associated with surgery; after surgery, there is the risk of infection of the wound. An artificial valve has the risk of blood clots forming on it, which can lead to a blood clot forming in a blood vessel and stop blood reaching tissues

C there are more people needing a transplant than available organs; the donor organ has to be tissue matched to the recipient so it is not rejected; for some other transplants, such as kidney, the organ can come from a relative who is more likely to be a close tissue match; this is not possible for heart transplants

B4.5

A ribs, diaphragm, trachea, area, capillaries, oxygen, blood

B clockwise from left: lungs, trachea, bronchi, bronchiole, alveoli

C carbon dioxide: 4; nitrogen: 80; oxygen: 20

D **a** the alveoli are surrounded with capillaries

b the alveoli have a spherical shape and there are lots of them

c ventilation moves air in and out of the alveoli; the good blood supply removes oxygen and brings lots of carbon dioxide

d the alveoli have very thin walls which gives a short distance between air and the blood

B4.6

A roots, photosynthesis, epidermis, stomata, stem

B anticlockwise from top: upper epidermis, palisade mesophyll, spongy mesophyll, lower epidermis, guard cells, stomata, air space, vascular bundle

C epidermal tissues are often waterproof to reduce water loss; palisade mesophyll tissue contains lots of chloroplasts, which carry out photosynthesis; spongy mesophyll tissue contains some chloroplasts for photosynthesis but also has big air spaces and a large surface area to make the diffusion of gases easier; xylem carries water needed for photosynthesis from the roots up to the leaves; phloem carries dissolved food produced during photosynthesis from the leaves around the plant; lower epidermis contains stomata, through which carbon dioxide enters the leaf for photosynthesis

D $1\,m = 1\,000\,000\,\mu m$

$\dfrac{1\,000\,000}{100} = 10\,000$

$= 4$ orders of magnitude

B4.7

A xylem, roots, leaves, phloem, energy, protein / amino acids

B water – transported in xylem vessels, from root to leaves; mineral ions – dissolved in water, transported in xylem vessels, from root to leaves; sugars – transported in phloem vessels, from leaves to all parts of the plants

C **a** translocation

b it moves sugars from the leaves (where they are made during photosynthesis) to all other regions of the plant; the sugar is needed by cells to release energy during respiration

D **a** blue dots inside the stem

b the dots are the xylem vessels within vascular bundles that run up and down the stem; water had been taken up the stem via the xylem, which was then dyed by the food colouring

B4.8

A transpiration, leaf, guard, carbon dioxide, water, xylem

B water vapour – diffused out of the leaf
oxygen – diffused out of the leaf
carbon dioxide – diffused into the leaf

C water moves from the soil into the roots by osmosis; it moves from the roots into xylem vessels in the stem; it moves up the xylem vessels in the stem and enters into the leaves; water diffuses from the xylem vessels in the leaf through the air spaces in the spongy mesophyll; it evaporates from the leaves into the air through the stomata; this process is called transpiration

D $\dfrac{70}{0.05} = 1400$

$1400 \times 6 = 8400$

B4.9

A increase, carbon dioxide, water vapour, light, temperature, potometer, faster

B potometer

C **a** use a lamp; change the distance between the lamp and the potometer

b $2.4\,cm = 24\,mm$; $\dfrac{24}{4} = 6$ (mm/min)

c as the light intensity increases, the rate of transpiration increases; the rate of transpiration is higher in windy air than still air

B4 Practice questions

01.1 capillary [1]

01.2 its diameter is only slightly bigger than the red blood cell [1]

01.3 $\dfrac{1}{1.4} = 0.7$ [1] mm/s [1]

02.1 blood flow to heart muscle reduced; [1] muscle receiving less oxygen / glucose; [1] cells not able to respire efficiently (and release energy); [1] heart contraction is not effective [1]

02.2 **a** stent: small balloon added into artery and inflated; [1] wire mesh tube added into artery [1]
heart bypass: small piece of blood vessel taken from elsewhere in the body; [1] joined to coronary artery around the blockage to provide an alternative route for the blood [1]

b advantages of a stent: **two** from: only requires keyhole surgery so wound is very small; [1] only requires a local anaesthetic – fewer risks than general; [1] patient is able to resume with normal daily activities quickly after surgery; [1] surgery is quick and relatively cheap [1]
disadvantage of a stent: cannot be used for badly blocked arteries [1]
advantages of bypass surgery: **one** or **two** from: can be used where the blockage cannot be helped with stents; [1] can be used where the patient has many blockages [1]
disadvantages of bypass surgery: **one** or **two** from: requires a general anaesthetic which carries risks; [1] long, expensive surgery; [1] risk of infection of wound; [1] recovery is long [1]

B5.1

A mental, infectious, microorganisms / pathogens, non-communicable, diet

B **a** common cold / flu

b asthma **c** type 2 diabetes

C obesity – eating too much food causes the body to store the excess as fat;
HIV/AIDS – the virus can be passed from person to person by sharing infected needles;
diarrhoea-linked diseases – drinking water is not treated so there are pathogens in it which cause the diseases

D **a** graph can be any shape as long as it is showing a positive relationship with line extending from y-axis

b to improve the quality of their data they should increase the sample size so it is larger than 100; they could also use a way of measuring stress levels, e.g. heart rate or adrenaline levels in the blood, rather than relying on people to report how they feel, which is not an accurate indication of stress

B5.2

A microorganisms, viruses, toxins, viruses, air

B **two** from: viruses are much smaller than bacteria; viruses reproduce inside cells, bacteria reproduce outside cells; viruses are always pathogens, many species of bacteria are not pathogens; bacteria are living cells, viruses are non-living

C viruses infect cells; they replicate inside and burst open the cells when they escape

D **a** his body is responding to the cell damage and toxins produced by the bacteria (the body raises the temperature to slow down the growth of the bacteria)

b the bacteria are damaging the cells that line his throat / producing toxins that affect the cells

E common cold – **by the air, in water droplets**; HIV/AIDS – **direct sexual contact or exchange of blood**; cholera – **in the water**

B5.3

A antibiotics / antiseptics, Petri, agar, nutrient, inoculating, microorganisms, 25 °C

B **a** holds the agar gel
b contains nutrients for bacterial growth
c transfers bacteria to the agar gel
d a warm place to increase the growth rate of the bacteria

C **a** the Petri dishes are sterilised before use; glass dishes can be sterilised by heating in an autoclave; plastic Petri dishes are bought ready-sterilised (where UV light or gamma radiation is used to kill the bacteria); the nutrient agar is also sterilised by heating it
b a Bunsen burner is placed near to the agar dish to kill any bacteria that may fall from the air onto the dish; the inoculating loop is sterilised by placing it into a blue Bunsen burner flame; the lid of the agar dish is tilted up slightly, not fully removed; the plate is inoculated as quickly as possible
c the Petri dishes have lids; the lids are fixed to the plate using tape

D **a** to prevent the growth of harmful (pathogenic) bacteria
b to increase the rate of growth of the bacteria

B5.4

A division, nutrients / food, antiseptics, antibiotics, inhibition, larger / bigger

B **a** $\frac{60}{20} = 3$ divisions an hour
4 hours × 3 = 12 (divisions)
b $10 \times 2^{12} = 40\,960$

C **a** 30 minutes
b no, because the bacteria will run out of food / nutrients in the agar; their growth would slow down; eventually the numbers will decrease as the bacteria die

B5.5

A pathogens / microorganisms, spread, washing, vectors

B observation, hypothesis, method, results, conclusion

C microscope; it helped because scientists could study diseased tissue and see the microorganisms (they are too small to be seen with the naked eye)

D common cold – cover mouth when coughing or sneezing; *Salmonella* (food poisoning) – make sure food is properly cooked before eating it

B5.6

A measles, vaccine, immune / white blood, AIDS, direct, blood, mosaic, vectors, photosynthesis

B **a** **two** from: by sexual contact; sharing needles or blood transfusions; from mother to baby during pregnancy, breast feeding or during birth
b **two** from: using condoms during sex; not sharing needles for drug use; screening blood for the virus before being used for blood transfusions; education

C **a** between 1965 and 2005 the number of people infected with measles has decreased
b a vaccination programme was introduced so more people are immune to measles and do not catch it

D **a** the plants will not be able to carry out photosynthesis as effectively so will not be able to make their food
b remove the infected plants from the greenhouse. Use an insecticide to kill insects which may act as vectors

B5.7

A bacteria, toxins, vaccinated, sexually, penis, antibiotics, condoms, plants, cells

B **a** vomiting and diarrhoea
b discharge from vagina or penis
c mass of cells on the plant's shoot (crown gall)

C **three** from: not washing raw chicken, because the spray from the water may contain bacteria and contaminate nearby surfaces [UK government advice]; use separate chopping boards / utensils for the raw chicken and the salad, because bacteria on the raw chicken may be transferred to the salad, which will not be cooked; keep the raw chicken and salad separate; wash hands after handling the raw chicken; make sure the chicken is cooked all the way through (so no pink bits remain) – this will ensure that all bacteria are killed

D **a** by direct contact during sex
b strains have evolved that are resistant to many antibiotics

B5.8

A fungi, photosynthesis, malaria, liver, nets, blood

B **a** the leaf is roughly a circle with a radius of 20 mm;
area of a circle = $\pi r^2 = 3 \times 20^2 = 1200$ mm²
b each spot is roughly a circle with a radius of 5 mm; area = $\pi r^2 = 3 \times 5^2 = 75$ mm²;
there are 3 spots: 75 × 3 = total area of 225 mm²
$\frac{225}{1200} \times 100 = 18.75\%$

C **a** the number of cases increased between 1971 and 2000; the number of cases decreased between 2000 and 2003
b the number of cases = 30 000; the number of deaths = 125; $\frac{125}{30\,000} \times 100 = 0.42\%$

B5.9

A barrier, platelets, trachea, mucus, cilia, acid, food, blood, antibodies

B **a** the skin acts as a barrier and produces antimicrobial secretions to kill pathogens.; if it is cut, platelets help to form a clot that dries into a scab to seal it
b the stomach contains strong acid to kill any pathogens that enter the body in food

C the goblet cells produce mucus; pathogens get trapped in the mucus; ciliated cells have cilia on their surface; cilia waft the mucus and trapped pathogens away from the lungs to the back of the throat, where it is swallowed

D some white blood cells ingest pathogens; some white blood cells produce antibodies, which target pathogens and destroy them; some white blood cells produce antitoxins, which counteract the toxins released by bacteria

B5.10

A bacterial, aphids, phloem, vectors, nitrate, chlorophyll, chlorosis, fertilisers

B **a** they cannot be passed from plant to plant
b yellowing of the leaves called chlorosis
c the plant cannot make chlorophyll, so the rate of photosynthesis decreases

C **a** aphids pierce plant stems with their sharp mouthpieces and feed on the sap inside phloem vessels which contain sugar; aphids feed in huge numbers depriving the plant of the products of photosynthesis; plants cannot synthesise new tissues as effectively
aphids also act as vectors, transferring pathogens from diseased plants into the tissues of healthy plants, causing disease that damages tissues
b use chemical pesticides / insecticides to kill the aphids / use biological control – introduce other organisms that eat aphids, e.g. ladybirds

D the stunted growth is due to a lack of nitrates in the soil; nitrates are needed to make amino acids / proteins; the nitrates have been removed from the soil by the plants and not replaced, so the level decreases every year; the farmer should add a fertiliser high in nitrate to the soil; this can be an artificial chemical or a natural fertiliser, like manure

B5.11

A physical, cuticles, antibacterial, structural / mechanical, mimicry

B **two** from: cellulose cell wall acts as a barrier around cells; thick cuticle on leaves to provide a barrier; bark on trees and a thick layer of dead cells around the stem provide a barrier; producing antibacterial chemicals to kill bacteria

C **a** mimicry
b butterflies do not lay eggs on the leaves to avoid competition with other caterpillars; this protects the leaves from being eaten by caterpillars

D **similarities**: both produce chemicals to kill pathogens – humans produce acid in stomach and antimicrobial secretions from the skin, plants produce antibacterial chemicals; both use physical barriers – humans have the skin to prevent pathogens from entering the body, plants have cuticle on leaves, and dead cells around stems or bark **differences**: humans have an immune system which uses white blood cells to destroy pathogens; plants do not have an immune system; some plants (deciduous) can lose their infected leaves in autumn; humans cannot lose infected parts of their body

B5 Practice questions

01.1 a drug that kills bacteria [1]

01.2 independent variable: treatment; [1] dependent variable: the diameter of the sores after 30 days of treatment [1]

01.3 it was a control [1] to check that the antibiotics helped reduce the size of the sores [1]

01.4 antibiotic B was the most effective [1] because it reduced the diameter of the sore the most [1]

01.5 bar chart [1] because the independent variable (type of antibiotic) is categories / categoric [1]

02.1 they kill the protists in the blood [1] and stop the disease developing [1]

02.2 the eggs / larvae are killed [1] before they have a chance to grow into adults [1]

03.1 the clear circle with the largest area was around disinfectant **D**; [1] this shows that disinfectant **D** was the most effective at killing the bacteria; [1] disinfectant **A** did not kill the bacteria – it was the least effective; [1] the order of effectiveness, from most to least, was **D**, **B**, **C**, **A** [1]

03.2 $\frac{4.2\,\text{cm}}{2} = 2.1\,\text{cm}$ [1]

$\pi \times 2.1^2 = 14\ (\text{cm}^2)$ (to 2 s.f.) [1]

B6.1

A antigens, vaccine, antibodies, white, herd

B clockwise from top: pathogen, antibody, white blood cell, antigen

C white blood cells are stimulated to produce the correct antibodies against the inactive bacteria; memory white blood cells 'remember' the right antibody; the person is immune to the disease; if live tetanus bacteria infect the body, white blood cells respond rapidly and make the right antibodies; antibodies attack and destroy the live bacteria; the live tetanus bacteria are destroyed before they can multiply and cause symptoms of the disease

D as the number of people being vaccinated increased, the number of cases of measles decreased; this is evidence to support vaccination helping to prevent the spread of measles

B6.2

A painkillers, antibiotics, resistant, viruses, cells

B antibiotic: to kill the bacteria causing the infection/to cure the infection; painkiller: to reduce the pain caused by the infection

C **a** doctors and vets could not give out antibiotics routinely – only for severe cases of infection

b discover / develop new antibiotics

D **a** the higher the concentration of antibiotic, the bigger the inhibition zone; so, the higher the concentration, the more bacteria were killed

b repeatability: repeat the experiment using another culture plate and check the results are similar; reproducibility: get another scientist to repeat the experiment and check results are similar

B6.3

A plants, fungi / mould, antibiotic, Fleming

B aspirin contains a higher concentration of salicylic acid than willow bark, so is more effective; willow bark contains other compounds that may result in unwanted side-effects; the amount of salicylic acid in willow bark is unknown and may vary, a person may take too much which can cause health issues; the amount in aspirin is controlled so people know the dose of salicylic acid in each tablet

C the mould is producing a substance which kills bacteria / stops the growth of bacteria

D **a** to see if the drug is an effective antibiotic

b to check that the drug is not toxic to human cells

c to test if the drug works in whole organisms

B6.4

A years, safe, animals, trials, dose, blind, placebo, doctor

B efficacy: to see if the drug works to cure the illness; toxicity: to check that the drug is not harmful; dosage: to find out the correct amount of drug to use

C **a** to check that the drug is not harmful to living organisms

b to check for side effects

c to check that the drugs works to treat heart disease

D **a** a substance which does not contain the active drug

b a placebo was used as a control; the symptoms of the control group can be compared against the group that took the drug to see if the drug has any effect; the sample size was quite small (only 220 people); a larger group would give more valid data; the efficacy of the drug was tested by asking the volunteers how they felt; this will not provide accurate data as people perceive their symptoms differently (it is subjective)

B6.5

A lymphocytes, tumour, hybridoma, purified, pregnancy

B lymphocytes produce many antibodies but cannot divide; tumour cells can divide repeatedly; hybridoma cells can produce antibodies and divide repeatedly in order to produce monoclonal antibodies

C from the top, clockwise: lymphocytes, tumour cells, hybridoma cells, monoclonal antibodies

D **a** blood clots can form in blood vessels, blocking blood from reaching cells; cells can't respire without oxygen and nutrients and die; this may damage an organ

b monoclonal antibodies have been developed to bind only to the clotting proteins; the antibodies have markers attached to them.; they bind to the antigens on the blood clots; the location of the markers can be detected using a camera outside of the body

B6.6

A antigens, toxic, dividing, cells, side

B **a** the cancer cells are also body cells; the treatments cannot distinguish between cancer cells and healthy body cells, so they destroy both

b from the top down: monoclonal antibody, cancer cell, antigens

c **one** from: triggering immune response, so immune system destroys cancer cells; blocking receptors on the surface of cancer cells and so stop growth stimulating molecule from binding to the cells and stop them growing and dividing; carrying toxic drugs, radioactive substances, or chemicals that stop cells growing and dividing to attack the cancer cells directly

d they only bind to the specific diseased or damaged cells that need treatment; healthy cells are not affected

C initially they created more side effects than expected; the monoclonal antibodies produced were mouse antibodies, and they triggered an immune response in humans; producing the right monoclonal antibodies and attaching them to drugs and other compounds proved more difficult than expected

B6 Practice questions

01.1 flu is caused by a virus; [1] antibiotics only kill bacteria [1]

01.2 vaccine contains dead / inactive pathogens / viruses; [1] white blood cells produce antibodies; [1] memory cells 'remember' the antibody; [1] if body is infected with live virus, antibodies are made quickly [1]

01.3 the percentage increased [1]

01.4 $7.8 \times \frac{64}{100} = 4.992 = 5$ million (people) [3]

01.5 the virus is not able to infect as many people [1] so it does not spread in the population [1]

02 new drugs help save lives / improve life quality; [1] we have a duty to provide care for unwell people; [1] drugs are tested on animals, which causes them to suffer; [1] drugs are tested on human volunteers, and can cause dangerous side-effects [1]

B7.1

A passed, risk, increased, diabetes, causal, lung

B **a** skin cancer; any inherited condition, e.g. cystic fibrosis / polydactyly / breast cancer; obesity / type 2 diabetes; lung cancer / heart disease (CVD) / emphysema / COPD / bronchitis

b UV light from the sun; overeating / smoking cigarettes; your genes

C **a** P **b** R **c** Q and S

D **a** as foot length increases, so does the ability to do mental arithmetic

b the older children have larger feet, and have had more practice at doing mental arithmetic

B7.2

A cell, benign, malignant, secondary, UV, radiation, chemotherapy

B **a** normal cells – paler cells either side of central section; tumour cells – darker cells in centre of diagram

b **two** from: tumour cells grow uncontrolled / normal cells grow in a controlled way; tumour cells live longer / or converse; tumour cells divide more rapidly / or converse

C both are caused by uncontrolled cell division and can be life threatening; they can interfere with the normal function of a tissue / organ; malignant tumours (cancer) spread around the body, and they can form secondary tumours in different areas; this makes them more difficult to treat and control; benign tumours are contained in one place and cannot spread; this makes it easier for them to be treated, as once they are removed they no longer affect the organ

D **a** radiation is used to stop the cancer cells dividing

b the radiation can also damage healthy cells

B7.3

A nicotine, monoxide, tar, heart, lung, bronchitis, oxygen, birth weight

B **a** tar **b** nicotine
c carbon monoxide **d** tar

C smoking cigarettes increases your risk of developing lung cancer; however, it is possible to smoke and not develop lung cancer; the more cigarettes a person smokes per day, the higher their risk of developing lung cancer

D **a** 802 – 572 = 230 per 100 000 men per year

b $\frac{1025}{100\,000} \times 100 = 1\%$

B7.4

A overweight / obese, diabetes, blood, exercise, fatty, heart

B as a person ages, their metabolic rate slows down; their body does not use as much energy from food; they still may be eating the same amount of food; excess food, not used for energy, is stored as fat; this makes the person overweight; also, as a person ages they may not do so much physical activity, so not so much energy is transferred in this way

C exercise increases muscle tissue, which increases metabolic rate; this means that more energy from food is used the excess food is not stored as fat, so the person stays at a healthy weight; being overweight is a risk factor for illnesses such as high blood pressure and type 2 diabetes; exercise lowers blood cholesterol levels, which reduces the risk of fatty deposits building on arteries; this lowers the risk of developing heart disease

D in both men and women, the higher a person's BMI index, the higher their risk of developing type 2 diabetes; overweight and obese women have a higher risk than men of the same BMI

B7.5

A nervous, slows, coma, liver, pregnant, mutations, sun, skin

B **a** liver, brain

b between 1991 and 2008 the number of alcohol-related deaths in the UK has increased; from 9 per 100 000 of the population to 19 per 100 000 of the population

C **a** it is a form of ionising radiation, which is breathed into the lungs; here it penetrates the cells, damaging the DNA and causing mutations

b £1000 + (£2 × 52) = **£1104**

c data from scientific research; this should be carried out by independent researchers (not funded by the company so it is not biased); the research should be peer-reviewed and published in a scientific journal

B7 Practice questions

01.1 a group of cells that are dividing rapidly [1]

01.2 a disease that cannot be passed from person to person [1]

02.1 **three** from: the more cigarettes a person smokes, the higher their risk of developing mouth cancer; [1] the more alcohol a person drinks, the higher their risk of developing mouth cancer; [1] the risk of developing mouth cancer in people who smoke over 40 cigarettes a day is greatly increased (by around 5 times) if they drink 4 or more alcoholic drinks a day; [1] in people who smoke over 40 cigarettes a day the risk of developing mouth cancer

is slightly decreased if they drink 1–3 alcoholic drinks per day [1]

02.2 D, A, B, E, C [2 – 1 mark if 2 or 3 are in the correct place]

02.3 **one** from: the patient might not tell the truth; [1] the patient might not be monitoring how much they smoke and drink [1]

03.1 the higher the volume of alcohol drunk per day, the more likely there are to be tumour cells [1]

03.2 **advantages**: other variables that affect the development of mouth cancer can be controlled; [1] it is not ethical to give humans alcohol in an attempt to cause cancer; [1] **disadvantages**: results may not be valid [1] because alcohol may affect rats differently to humans [1]

B8.1

A endothermic, algae, light, water, chlorophyll, glucose

B

$$\text{carbon dioxide} + \textbf{water} \xrightarrow{\textbf{light}} \text{glucose} + \textbf{oxygen}$$

$$6\,\textbf{CO}_2 + 6H_2O \longrightarrow \textbf{C}_6\textbf{H}_{12}\textbf{O}_6 + 6O_2$$

C add a glowing splint to the test tube; if it relights, oxygen is present

D **a** increases the surface area for light to fall on

b brings water to the cells to be used for photosynthesis, carries glucose away to other cells in the plant

c so the diffusion distance for gases is short

B8.2

A light, carbon dioxide, limiting, brighter, increases, enzymes, increase

B **a** light intensity

b the volume of oxygen / number of bubbles produced in a certain time

c **two** from: the temperature of the water; type of plant; temperature of room; concentration of carbon dioxide in the water

C as the distance increased by 10 cm, the light intensity decreased by a factor of 0.01 $\left(\frac{1}{10^2}\right)$

D

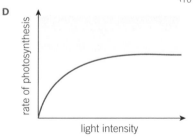

E carbon dioxide concentration; temperature; chlorophyll levels in the leaf

B8.3

A respiration, starch, cellulose, nitrate, proteins

B **a** to soften the cuticle so the iodine can be absorbed into the leaf

b because ethanol is flammable; it is a hazard to use it near naked flames

c to remove the green chlorophyll from the leaf so the change in colour when the iodine is added can be clearly seen

C **Leaf A**: result: whole leaf is coloured blue/black; explanation: the cells in the leaf have been exposed to light so have carried out photosynthesis and stored the glucose as starch; the blue/black colour is a positive result for starch

Leaf B: result: the leaf, apart from the strip in the middle, is coloured blue/black; explanation: the middle section of the leaf was covered by a piece of black paper; light could not get to these sections so the cells here could not carry out photosynthesis and make starch

Leaf C: result: only the green areas are coloured blue/black; explanation: the green areas contain chlorophyll, which is needed for photosynthesis; the cells in the white areas have no chlorophyll so cannot carry out photosynthesis

D **four** from: to carry out respiration (and transfer energy from glucose); to make lipids; to make proteins; to build cellulose (for cell walls); to store as starch

B8.4

A carbon dioxide, photosynthesis, grow, hydroponics, optimum

B **ventilation vents**: used to control the temperature of the greenhouse, so it does not get too hot; if plants get too hot then the rate of photosynthesis will decrease because enzymes are denatured

paraffin heater: used to increase the temperature to increase the rate of photosynthesis; temperature is a limiting factor, if it is not warm enough then it will limit the rate of photosynthesis; it also releases carbon dioxide into the greenhouse; the concentration of carbon dioxide in the air is also a limiting factor for photosynthesis

automatic watering system: this will water the plants when the soil gets dry; it will make sure that there is enough water for photosynthesis (because amount of water is a limiting factor), but will ensure that the soil does not get waterlogged

automatic lights: these will come on when it is dark so the plants get a high light intensity at all time; light intensity is a limiting factor for photosynthesis, if it is not high enough then the rate of photosynthesis will be limited

C **a** high light intensity, a temperature of 30 °C, high carbon dioxide

b using a temperature of 30 °C will increase the rate of photosynthesis, and the growth of his plants but it will also increase the cost of running the greenhouse; the amount of profit will be greater if he uses 20 °C

B8 Practice questions

01.1 light intensity [1]

01.2 it absorbs the heat from the lamp [1] to control the temperature [1]

01.3 $\dfrac{1}{0.10}$ [1] = 100 [1]

01.4 as the distance between the lamp and the pondweed decreased, the number of gas bubbles produced in 1 minute increased [1] up to 0.10 m; [1] after this distance, the number of bubbles stayed the same [1]

01.5 as the distance between the lamp and the pondweed decreased, the light intensity increased; [1] the plant received more light, so carried out photosynthesis at a faster rate; [1] at a distance of 0.10 m, decreasing the distance does not increase the rate of photosynthesis [1] because something else is limiting the rate, e.g. carbon dioxide concentration [1]

01.6 the measurement of volume of oxygen produced is not accurate; [1] the results are affected by random errors; [1] measure the volume of oxygen produced (rather than count bubbles); [1] use a measuring cylinder / gas syringe to collect gas and measure the volume; [1] repeat the measurements (to reduce the effect of random errors) [1]

B9.1

A exothermic, oxygen, carbon dioxide, mitochondria, energy

B **a** word equation:
glucose + oxygen → water + carbon dioxide
balanced symbol equation:
$$C_6H_{12}O_6 + 6O_2 \rightarrow 6H_2O + 6CO_2$$

b energy is not a substance; only substances are included in a word equation.

C her body contains more muscle cells; muscle cells contain many mitochondria, for respiration, so they can carry out movement; she has more mitochondria so carries out respiration at a higher rate when at rest; she needs more food to provide glucose for respiration

D **a** to move the tail, so it can travel to the egg and fertilise it

b for active transport, to move mineral ions from the soil into the plant

B9.2

A muscles, heart, glycogen, blood, oxygen, carbon dioxide

B **a** the breathing rate and the volume of air taken in and out of the lungs increase; the glycogen stored in your muscles is converted to glucose

b to increase the flow of oxygenated blood to the muscles; this enables the rate of respiration to increase in the muscle cells so more energy for movement can be transferred; also, it increases the removal of carbon dioxide (which is made during respiration) from the muscle cells

C she has confused breathing and respiration; she should have said 'The rate of respiration increases, to transfer more energy from glucose; the rate of breathing increases to bring more oxygen to the cells.'

D the pulse rate of all students increased during exercise; Jasmine's pulse rate increased the most (by 82 beats per minute) – she was the least fit; Ruby's pulse rate increased the least (by 74 beats per minute) – she was the fittest

B9.3

A oxygen, oxygen, debt, ethanol

B lactic acid; ethanol + carbon dioxide

C in both, glucose is used as a reactant, and energy is transferred to the environment; aerobic: oxygen is reacted with glucose; anaerobic: oxygen is not a reactant; aerobic: carbon dioxide is produced as a waste product; anaerobic: lactic acid is a waste product; aerobic respiration transfers more energy than anaerobic respiration, because glucose is fully oxidised in aerobic respiration but only partially oxidised in anaerobic respiration; aerobic respiration occurs continuously in cells, anaerobic respiration only occurs when the cell does not have enough oxygen to carry our aerobic respiration, e.g. during intense exercise.

D **a** unfit: 4 minutes; fit: 2.5 minutes

b to breakdown the lactic acid produced during anaerobic respiration into carbon dioxide and water so it can be removed from the body; it requires oxygen (the oxygen debt); so breathing remains high to supply the oxygen needed

c the fit person has a quicker recovery time than the unfit person because they have a bigger heart and lungs with a better blood supply, so the oxygen needed for the oxygen debt gets to cells more quickly

B9.4

A respiration, glucose, amino, urea, liver, anaerobic, glucose

B the sum of all the chemical reactions in your body

C **a** respiration **b** photosynthesis

D blood flowing through the muscles picks up lactic acid and transports it to the liver; lactic acid is converted into glucose; the glucose is used in aerobic respiration, or stored in the liver as glycogen

B9 Practice questions

01.1 ethanol [1]

01.2 measure the volume of carbon dioxide produced [1]

01.3 the gas syringe is already pushed out; [1] if it is not pushed in then the volume of carbon dioxide produced will not be measured accurately [1]

01.4 change the temperature of the yeast by placing the flask in water bath at different temperatures; [1] measure the volume of gas (carbon dioxide) produced [1] over a certain time OR time how long it takes for a certain volume of gas to be produced; [1] at least one control variable mentioned, e.g. mass of yeast, volume of glucose solution / concentration of glucose solution / room temperature [1]

01.5 between 20 °C and around 37 °C, the rate increased as the temperature increased; [1] between around 37 °C and 42 °C, the rate stayed around constant; [1] between around 42 °C and 50 °C, the rate decreased as the temperature increased; [1] it supports the student's prediction only up to 37 °C [1]

01.6 respiration is catalysed by enzymes; [1] at high temperatures, the enzyme denatures; [1] the reactant (glucose) is no longer able to fit in the active site [1]

B10.1

A internal, glucose, hormonal, receptors

B blood glucose concentration; body temperature; water content of the body / blood

C his body temperature **increases** because his muscles are carrying out respiration at a faster rate to transfer energy to use for movement; some energy is transferred as heat; his blood water level **decreases** because he is producing sweat in order to lower his body temperature; his blood glucose level **decreases** because he is using glucose in respiration in his muscle cells to release energy for movement

D a receptors **b** coordination centre
 c effectors

B10.2

A electrical / nervous, stimuli, sensory, spinal, motor, muscles

B from top to bottom: eye – light; ear – sound and change in position; nose – chemical; skin – change in temperature / pressure / pain

C **electrical impulses** are sent along **sensory neurones** until they reach the central nervous system (**CNS**, which consists of the brain and spinal cord); the CNS coordinates the response and sends impulses out along **motor neurones** to the arm **muscles**, which are **effectors**; these contract to move the arms towards the ball

D a **A**: sensory **B**: motor
 b arrow going from left to right along each neurone

B10.3

A automatic, brain, harm, relay, effector, synapses, chemicals

B a they are involuntary – they happen without you knowing because the conscious parts of the brain is not involved

 b speed = $\dfrac{\text{distance}}{\text{time}}$

 $120 = \dfrac{3}{\text{time}}$

 time $= \dfrac{3}{120} = 0.025\,\text{s}$

 c to protect the body from harm, for example, getting burnt

C sensory neurone **W**, motor neurone **V**, relay neurone **U**, receptor **Y**, effector **X**, synapse **Z**

D a synapse
 b chemicals are released from neurone **C**; they diffuse across the gap / synapse; they bind with receptors on neurone **D**

B10.4

A neurones, medulla, hypothalamus, hormones, MRI

B medulla – Z – unconscious activities, such as controlling the heartbeat, the movements of the gut, and breathing
cerebral cortex – X – consciousness, intelligence, memory, and language
cerebellum – Y – coordinating muscular activity and balance

C a the brain is inside the skull; it is very delicate and easily damaged
 b it is very complex so difficult to investigate the effects of drugs; drugs are not always able to pass through the membranes which surround the brain; it is easy to cause damage during surgery

D it can be carried out without having to remove part of the skull, so no risk of damaging the brain; it can show what areas of the brain are activated when carrying out different tasks, allowing scientists to see what areas of the brain are damaged; it is simple to carry out, with no need for surgery

B10.5

A retina, sclera, cornea, focuses, pupil, lens, optic, brain

B **A** – iris; **B** – retina; **C** – optic nerve; **D** – cornea; **E** – pupil

C a optic nerve
 b top label: sensory (neurone), bottom label: motor (neurone)
 c bright light detected by retina; impulses sent along sensory neurone (through optic nerve) to the brain / CNS; impulses sent to iris muscles along motor neurones; iris muscles contract to increase the size of the iris / reduce the size of the pupil; less light enters pupil
 d to reduce the amount of light entering the eye to protect the retina

D light rays enter the eye through the cornea, where they are bent (refracted) a little; they then travel through the pupil and the lens, where they are refracted further in order to meet on the retina and form an upside down image

B10.6

A lens, contract, thicker, distant / far, ciliary, tight, contact

B the process of changing the shape of the lens in the eye, to ensure that an image is formed on the retina.

C light from the distant object is almost parallel; the ciliary muscles relax so the suspensory ligaments tighten; the lens is pulled flatter to refract the light rays slightly so they are focused on the retina

D a myopia / short sightedness
 b the light is focused in front of the retina so a clear image is not formed / image is blurred
 c light rays are drawn on the diagram as straight lines; they meet on the retina

B10 Practice questions

01.1 trial 1 [1] example of random error: e.g. one of the students losing concentration [1]

01.2 $\dfrac{(5.0 + 4.8 + 4.7)}{3}$ [1] = 4.8 (s) [1]

01.3 $\dfrac{4.8}{6}$ [1] = 0.8 (s) [1]

01.4 repeat the experiment [1] until the time taken is similar for each repeat [1]

01.5 **one** from: use the ruler drop test; [1] use a digital reaction timer / computer program [1]

02.1 in hyperopia, distant objects appear clear but close objects appear blurred; [1] in normal vision, objects both close and distant appear clear [1]

02.2 **one** from: lens too flat / thin; [1] short eyeball [1]

02.3 **one** advantage from: contact lenses are more suitable when playing sport; [1] contact lenses cannot be seen [1]
one disadvantage from: multi-use contact lenses have to be cleaned every night to keep them sterile; [1] single-use contact lenses are thrown away each day, adding to landfill; [1] contact lenses are more expensive; [1] contact lenses may cause eye infections if not sterilised properly [1]

B11.1

A hormonal / endocrine, hormones, target, nervous, master

B R – **pituitary gland** – FSH (in women); S – **thyroid gland** – thyroxine; T – adrenal gland – **adrenaline**; U – **pancreas** – insulin; V – **ovary (female)** – oestrogen; W – testis (male) – **testosterone**

C **two** from: most hormonal responses are slower than nervous ones; hormonal responses are transmitted by chemicals; hormonal effects are usually longer lasting than nervous ones; nervous responses are transmitted by electrical impulse

D it secretes hormones that affect other glands

B11.2

A pancreas, insulin, glycogen, glucagon, blood / bloodstream, negative, 1, 2

B glycogen: a storage carbohydrate found in the liver and muscles; glucose: the sugar used in respiration; glucagon: A hormone used to convert glycogen into glucose

C left: the pancreas secretes glucagon into the bloodstream; right: glucose moves from the blood into the cells to be used or stored as glycogen in the liver and muscle cells

D a they do not release insulin from their pancreas so have to inject it in order to lower blood glucose levels when they get too high

b glucose that is not used in respiration is stored as fat; if a person has too much fat stored on their body they will be obese

B11.3

A insulin, carbohydrates, exercise, drugs

B a X

b their blood glucose level went up higher than person **Y**; it took more time to come back down to the starting level

C the blood glucose levels of a person with type 1 diabetes can be controlled using insulin and changes to their diet so it does not rise too high or too low; but, they will always have the illness because the cells in their pancreas are damaged and this cannot be reversed

D it is likely that type 1 diabetes has a genetic element; so, the baby may also develop it; in the future, it may be possible to genetically engineer the stem cells to make functioning pancreas cells; that can be implanted into the baby's pancreas with no rejection issues; these will replace the faulty pancreas cells so the pancreas can produce insulin

B11.4

A thyroxine, metabolic, adrenal, oxygen, flight, negative

B a pituitary gland

b if thyroxine levels increase, the hormone inhibits the release of TSH, so the release of thyroxine is stopped; this is negative feedback; if thyroxine levels fall, release of TSH is no longer inhibited, so it is released; it stimulates the release of thyroxine from the thyroid gland; thyroxine levels rise again

C adrenaline is released from his adrenal glands; this travels in the blood to its target organs; heart and breathing rate increase to increase the delivery of oxygen and glucose to the muscles; stored glycogen in the liver is converted to glucose; blood is diverted from the digestive system to the muscles; this increases respiration in the muscles and prepares the body for fight or flight; (pupils dilate and there is also an increase in mental awareness)

B11.5

A puberty, sexual, ovaries, ovulation, menstrual, follicle, progesterone, testosterone, testes

B clockwise from top: fallopian tube / oviduct, uterus, vagina, cervix, ovary

C a sperm duct **b** scrotum
c testes **d** penis

D a X – oestrogen; Y – progesterone
b ovary
c in the blood / bloodstream / plasma
d **two** from: the breasts develop; fat is deposited on the hips, buttocks, and thighs; mature ova start to form every month in the ovaries; the uterus grows and becomes active; menstruation begins

B11.6

A pituitary, oestrogen, oestrogen, uterus, FSH, ovulation, progesterone

B a day 14 **b** days 6–14 **c** days 14–28

C during **days 0–5**, levels of FSH are high – this causes a new egg to mature in the ovary; oestrogen levels increase during **days 6–12** – this causes the thickness of the womb lining to increase, stimulates the release of LH from the ovaries, and stops the release of FSH; at **day 14**, levels of LH are at their highest – LH causes an egg to be released from an ovary (ovulation); between **days 14 and 24**, the lining of the uterus is maintained by high levels of progesterone – this also stops the release of FSH and LH

D it maintains the lining of the uterus, which the embryo is implanted into; it prevents FSH being released and another egg being released from the ovary, so another pregnancy cannot occur

B11.7

A sperm, uterus, pill, sperm, barrier, condoms, abstinence

B a the progesterone inhibits the production and release of FSH by the pituitary gland so no eggs mature
b advantage: very effective / lasts for up to 3 years; disadvantage: needs to be inserted by a doctor / slight risk of side-effects / does not protect against sexually transmitted infections (STIs)

C a diaphragm **b** 100 − 25 = 75%
c 1500 × 0.85 = 1275 women; it is not an accurate number because the answer is based on the average proportion of women who would get pregnant

B11.8

A LH, ovulation, IVF, fertilised, uterus

B fertility drugs are used to increase the number of mature eggs in the ovaries; eggs are collected and placed in a Petri dish; sperm from the father is used to fertilise the eggs; the fertilised eggs are checked to make sure they are developing properly; one or two of the embryos are placed into the mother's uterus to develop into a baby

C ¼ of the pie chart is labelled 'multiple births'; ¾ of the pie chart is labelled 'single births'

D a unwanted embryos may be destroyed
b it is expensive (either to the couple or the NHS)
c it is emotionally and physically stressful for the couple / there are a large number of children waiting for foster care or adoption

B11.9

A light, auxin, towards, gravity, roots

B a so plant shoots grow towards light and receive enough light for photosynthesis, to make glucose / sugar.

b so the plant grows the correct way round – roots grow down into the soil so they anchor into the soil and take up water and mineral ions; shoots grow up out of the soil so they can receive light for photosynthesis

C a the stem and root are shaded on the lower surface only
b the shoot has grown upwards, away from the force of gravity; the root has grown down, towards the force of gravity

D in shoots, auxins promote cell growth – the cells on the lower surface grow more, causing the shoot to bend up; in roots, auxins inhibit cell growth – the cells on the upper surface grow more, causing the root to bend down

B11.10

A auxins, rooting, fruit, gibberellins, dormancy

B a it causes the plant to grow rapidly and uncontrollably
b the weeds compete with crop plants for resources (light, water, mineral ions) so the growth of the crops decreases, reducing the yield
c the auxin falls on the leaves of the plants; weeds normally have larger leaves than the crop plant, so the weeds absorb more of the auxin

C method should include:
a suitable sample size: take 10 cuttings from the same plant
an independent variable: dip the ends of five of them in hormone rooting power; do not use rooting powder on the other five
use of control variables: plant each cutting in a different pot, each containing the same soil; leave them in the same conditions (same amount of light and heat); water them the same amount daily
a suitable dependent variable: measure the height of the cuttings every day for a month
a prediction: the cuttings dipped in rooting powder will have increased in height more than those not dipped in rooting powder; this is because the rooting power promotes root growth; the cuttings with longer / more developed roots will be able to absorb more water from the soil, which is used in photosynthesis, so they will grow more

D a so the fruit is less likely to be damaged and will not arrive overripe if there are any delays
b they are placed in a warm storage area and ethene is added to the air

B11 Practice questions

01.1 testes / testis / testicle [1]

01.2 testosterone [1] triggers male secondary sexual characteristics to develop during puberty [1] and stimulates sperm production [1]

01.3 sperm would not be able to travel to the penis (and be released during sex) [1] fertilisation of an egg could not occur [1]

01.4 **four** (to include a mixture of advantages and disadvantages) from: it is nearly 100% effective; [1] it provides contraception with no risk of human error; [1] it only needs a local anaesthetic; [1] man needs some time afterwards to recover; [1] it is permanent; [1] it does not provide protection against sexually transmitted infections; [1] it has a cost to the NHS [1]

02.1 type 1; [1] **one** reason from: people with type 1 diabetes need to inject themselves with insulin; [1] type 1 doesn't produce any / enough insulin; [1] type 2 can be controlled with diet only; [1] type 2 is associated with obesity but Paul has a normal BMI [1]

02.2 insulin dose would be less [1] because he would use up blood glucose through exercise [1]

02.3 insulin injections work faster / go straight to bloodstream; [1] insulin in tablets is likely to be digested and broken down [1]

B12.1

A brain, skin, temperature, dilate / widen, heat, low, sweating, shivering

B **a** enzymes will denature, and stop working; chemical reactions inside the body will not take place at a fast enough rate for survival

   b receptors in the skin send impulses along neurones to the thermoregulatory centre; also temperature receptors in the thermoregulatory centre detect an increase in blood temperature; it sends impulses along neurones to the skin where mechanisms are carried out to decrease body temperature

   c sweating, vasodilation

C **a** sweating cools down the body because water evaporates, transferring energy away from the skin

   b during vasoconstriction, blood vessels that supply capillaries in the skin constrict

D your muscles are contracting (and relaxing), which requires a fast rate of respiration to supply them with energy; during respiration, which is an exothermic reaction, some energy raises the temperature of the body

B12.2

A lungs, water, mineral, urine

B urea – made in liver – by the breakdown of excess amino acids / protein – removed by kidneys via urine; carbon dioxide – made in all cells – by respiration – removed through exhalation in the lungs

C **a** it prevents too much water entering or leaving the cell by osmosis; if too much water enters then the cell will burst, if too much leaves then the cell will shrivel up (crenation) and no longer work as effectively

   b removal into urine by the kidneys

   c sweating

D **a** $1500 + 500 + 350 + 150 = 2500$

   $\dfrac{2500}{1000} = 2.5\,\mathrm{dm^3}$

   b $\dfrac{500}{2500} \times 100 = 20\%$

   c the volume of water lost through the skin would increase; the volume of water lost through the urine would decrease; the other volumes would remain around the same

B12.3

A water, filtering, water, urine, ADH, tubules

B clockwise from top left: liver, kidney, bladder

C **a** urea: there is a higher concentration of urea in the urine compared to the blood; this is because urea is a waste product which is added to urine by the kidneys so it can be removed from the blood glucose: there no glucose in the urine but some in the blood; this is because glucose is a useful substance (for respiration) so does not need to be removed from the body in the urine

   b $\dfrac{1000}{10} = 10$

   $0.05\,\mathrm{mg} \times 10 = 0.5\,\mathrm{mg}$

D receptor cells in the brain detect the concentration of solutes in the blood plasma; if the blood becomes too concentrated, the pituitary gland releases lots of ADH into the blood; this affects the kidney tubules so they reabsorb much more water; this results in a relatively small volume of very concentrated urine, and the concentration of solutes in the blood returns to normal levels; if the solute concentration becomes too dilute, less ADH is released into the blood; less water is reabsorbed in the kidney tubules, so a large volume of dilute urine is produced and the blood solute concentration returns back to normal

B12.4

A failure, transplant, dialysis, urea, constant

B **a** it restores the concentrations of dissolved substances in the blood to normal levels, so she can carry on with a normal life

   b one from: it takes a long time to complete, she has to be attached to it for hours, several times a week; she has to manage her diet carefully

C **A, E, C, D, B**

D **a** waste product: urea / excess mineral ions; useful substance: glucose / amino acids

   b the dialysis fluid contains the same concentration of glucose and mineral ions as the blood of a person without kidney disease; this ensures there is no net movement of glucose out of the blood but any excess ions are removed from the blood by diffusion; the dialysis fluid contains no urea; this makes a steep concentration gradient from the blood down to the fluid so urea is removed from the blood

B12.5

A donor, rejection, immune, tissue, immunosuppressant

B **a** a healthy kidney is taken out of a donor and put in the body of someone with kidney failure

   b you have two kidneys, and can survive without one; you cannot survive without a heart

C advantages: no need to use dialysis, can lead a more normal life; healthy kidney function disadvantages: the kidney might be rejected, have to take immunosuppressant drugs which can result in infections; the kidney will have to be replaced eventually and a new donor found

D **a** there are more people who need a kidney transplant than transplant operations taking place; this is because there are not enough donors

   b the gap between those who need a kidney transplant and the number of kidney transplant operations / available kidneys is widening

B12 Practice questions

01 excess water; [1] excess mineral ions [1]

02.1 diffusion: urea moves from a high concentration to low concentration; [1] osmosis: urea moves through a partially permeable membrane [1]

02.2 allows diffusion of urea; [1] maintains steep concentration gradient; [1] prevents urea moving from fluid back into the blood [1]

02.3 $550 \times 60 \times 4$ [1] $= 132\,000\,\mathrm{cm^3} = 132\,\mathrm{dm^3}$ [1]

02.4 same concentration of glucose in fluid and blood; [1] if higher in blood then glucose moves out of blood (into fluid); [1] if lower in blood then glucose moves into blood (out of fluid) [1]

03 **five** from: having dialysis is restrictive, sessions are long and frequent; [1] dialysis requires a special diet; [1] long term dialysis can damage the body; [1] dialysis is always available, patient will have to wait for a donor organ; [1] a kidney transplant means that the patient no longer needs dialysis; [1] a transplant is less expensive than long-term dialysis; [1] risk of rejection with transplant; [1] a patient who has had a transplant will need to take immunosuppressant drugs, risk of infection; [1] transplanted kidney will need to be replaced [1]

B13.1

A one, sex, identical, meiosis, sexual, variation

B sexual reproduction requires two parents, asexual requires only one; in sexual reproduction fertilisation is used, in asexual mitosis is used; in sexual reproduction, the offspring are genetically different to each other and the parents; in asexual reproduction, the offspring are genetically identical to each other and the parent

C a asexual **b** sexual **c** asexual

D a they have the same DNA / genes as their parent (they are clones)

b half of their DNA / genes come(s) from one parent, and half from the other parent; so they share DNA / genes with both parents

E

Advantage	Quick / no need to find a mate / always successful	Produces variation in the offspring
Disadvantage	Does not produce variation in the offspring	Energy is wasted because a mate has to be found to reproduce with / not always successful (fertilisation may not occur)

B13.2

A meiosis, two, divides, four, fertilisation, mitosis

B mitosis, meiosis, fertilisation, zygote

C

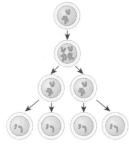

D skin cell – **46**; sperm cell – **23**; zygote – **46**; egg cell – **23**; ovary cell – **46**

B13.3

A natural, selective, asexual, both, sexually, human, spores, seeds, runners

B asexual reproduction involves one parent, sexual reproduction involves two; in asexual reproduction the offspring are clones of each other and their parent (they have the same genetic material); in sexual reproduction genetic material is mixed from both parents to create offspring that is genetically different to each other and the parents

C sexual reproduction: **advantages** – produces variation in the offspring; if the environment changes, this variation gives a survival advantage as some offspring will be able to survive and reproduce; **disadvantages** – takes time and energy to find a mate or spread gametes; it is often slower than asexual reproduction
asexual reproduction: **advantages** – time and energy efficient as there is no need to find a mate or spread gametes; often faster than sexual reproduction; offspring are identical, advantage in favourable conditions, because all offspring are adapted to survive; **disadvantage** – if environment changes then all offspring at risk and may not survive

D a joining of pollen and ovule during fertilisation to make seeds

b runners – new plants that form by mitosis on the end of existing stems

c reproduction will still occur if the flowers are destroyed by frost, eaten, or fail to be pollinated / new plants are dispersed more widely when seeds are scattered by animals who eat the fruit (and deposit the seeds)

B13.4

A polymer / molecule, double, chromosome, protein, genome

B the entire genetic material of an organism

C **W** – cell, **X** – nucleus, **Y** – chromosome, **Z** – gene

D a genome of a person with a rare disease can be compared to the genome of a relative; if the relative has the disease, scientists can look for genes / DNA sequences that are similar; if the relative does not have the disease, scientists can look for genes / DNA sequences that are different; these genes may be linked to disease; this means it is inherited

b if genes that are linked to diseases are identified then treatments can be developed; this could be using genetic engineering to change the gene

B13.5

A sugar, G, nucleotide, three, protein, carrier.

B circle labelled 'phosphate', pentagon labelled 'sugar', one section of a 'rung' labelled 'base', a group of a phosphate, sugar, and base labelled 'nucleotide'

C T, G, G, C, A, A, T

D a template is made from the gene; the template leaves the nucleus and joins to a ribosome in the cytoplasm; amino acids are brought to the template; each three bases codes for one amino acid; the amino acids are joined together to form a protein chain; the protein chain folds up to form a protein with a specific shape

B13.6

A proteins, genes, expressed, function, shape

B a DNA that does not code for a protein

b when a protein, coded for by a gene, is synthesised in a cell

c a change in the DNA

C testosterone is a protein; the gene that codes for testosterone is switched on; the protein is synthesised in the cells

D a the myostatin protein folds to give a different shape; it no longer has the same effect on muscle cells; muscle cell growth is not inhibited so they grow larger

b the animal will be stronger than others; it will be able to compete more effectively for resources, e.g. it will be faster to catch prey, able to fight others for a mate; this will make it more likely to survive and pass on its genes to its offspring

B13.7

A alleles, genotype, phenotype, same, heterozygous, dominant, recessive, two

B a Hh **b** HH **c** hh **d** Hh, HH

C a plant 1: white flowers; plant 2: yellow flowers

b

		Plant 1	
		t	t
Plant 2	T	**Tt**	**Tt**
	T	**Tt**	**Tt**

c yellow flowers

D

		Plant 1	
		T	t
Plant 2	T	**TT**	**Tt**
	t	**Tt**	**tt**

B13.8

A Punnett, phenotypes, ratios, 23, sex, X, males

B a red **b** 25% **or** 1 in 4

c 50% **or** 2 in 4 **or** 1 in 2

d 3 red : 1 orange **e** 1:1

C

		Mother	
		X	X
Father	X	XX	XX
	Y	XY	XY

the ratio of XX (female) to XY (male) is 1:1 / 50% are XX and 50% are XY

D person 6 and person 7 both have free earlobes but they have a son (person 10) who has attached earlobes; this means that they could both be carriers of the recessive allele and have passed on this allele to their son

B13.9

A inherited, polydactyly, dominant, mucus, recessive, both

B cystic fibrosis – **areas in the body get clogged up by thick mucus** – **two recessive alleles**
polydactyly – **extra fingers or toes** – **one dominant allele**

C a

		Mother	
		D	d
Father	d	**Dd**	**dd**
	d	**Dd**	**dd**

b no, it is likely, but not certain – each time they have a child there will be a 50% chance it will have polydactyly

D a they are both carriers for the disorder; they both passed one recessive allele to Maddy

b 25% **or** 1 in 4

B13.10

A fetuses, genes, villus, miscarriage, IVF, ethical

B chorionic villus sampling is carried out earlier in the pregnancy than amniocentesis; in both, a needle is inserted through the wall of the uterus but in chorionic villus sampling cells are taken from the placenta; in amniocentesis, cells are taken from the amniotic fluid; both carry a small risk of miscarriage.

C **a** eggs are collected and fertilised with sperm in a dish; they are left to develop into embryos; a cell is taken from each embryo and screened to see if it contains the affected gene; one or two healthy embryos are placed into the uterus to develop

   b embryos that have the gene for the condition are destroyed/people do not have the right to choose which embryos survive

B13 Practice questions

01.1 economic – **A**; [1] ethical – **D**; [1] can be answered by science – **B** [1]

01.2

	F	f
f	Ff	ff
f	Ff	ff

50% **or** 1 in 2; [1] genotypes correct for both parents; [1] genotypes correct for all offspring [1]

01.3 example answer – **six** from: there is a risk of miscarriage / harm to the fetus as a result of having the test; [1] results may not be accurate; [1] need to decide whether they would terminate a pregnancy; [1] moral / ethical considerations; [1] economic implications / stress on family of having a child with the condition; [1] quality of life for the child; [1] test results could reveal other information / issues / other disorders [1]

02 a change in the DNA may change a gene; [1] the change in a gene may change the sequence of amino acids coded for by the gene; [1] the shape of the protein formed may be altered; [1] changes in proteins may result in harmful changes to cell processes [1]

B14.1

A variation, genes, environmental, both, twins, genetics, environment

B just genetics: brown hair, green eyes, blood group A; just environment: scar, French accent, short hair, speaks English, speaks many languages; combination: mass, height, IQ

C **a** **three** from: amount / intensity / wavelength of light; concentration of carbon dioxide; concentration of minerals in the soil; temperature of surroundings; volume of water given to plant

   b change in height / mass / number of leaves on seedling

D **a** no

   b identical twins have the same genes; if type 1 diabetes was only due to genetics, if one twin had it then so would the other 100% of the time

B14.2

A natural, billion, mutations, environmental, breed / reproduce, fertile, species

B a change in the DNA code

C **mutation of a gene**: a few bacteria in a population have a new allele that makes them resistant to antibiotics; **advantage to survival**: antibiotics are used on the population; the resistant bacteria are not killed; **breed**: the resistant bacteria reproduce to form genetically identical offspring; **pass on genes**: the population of resistant bacteria increases; there are now more resistant bacteria than non-resistant ones

D **a** they will be able to see predators more quickly and escape before being eaten; they will be able to find more food

   b the mice with the better eyesight will survive to breed, and pass this characteristic onto their offspring

B14.3

A animals, breed, resistance, gentle, flowers, variation

B **two** from: large grains; many grains; short stalk (to prevent them being blown over by the wind); resistance to disease; resistance to insect attack

C select dogs that can run fast; breed them together; continue to do this for many generations

D **a** breeding together animals that are closely related

   b it results in little variation in the population; this increases the risk of certain diseases of inherited defects

B14.4

A engineering, genes, enzymes, vector, resistant, modified

B **a** **V**: insulin gene is cut out of human DNA using enzymes; **W**: a plasmid is removed from the bacteria and cut open using enzymes; **X**: insulin gene is joined to the plasmid using enzymes; **Y**: plasmid with insulin gene in it is taken up by the bacteria; **Z**: The gene is switched on and the bacteria start making insulin

   b the plasmid

C pest resistance, so crops do not get destroyed by pests, e.g. insects; increase in size of fruit or nutritional value of crop; increase ability to grow in difficult conditions, e.g. rice in flooded fields; disease resistance, so they do not get destroyed by pathogens; resistance to herbicides, so farmers can spray entire field with herbicides to kill weeds without damaging the crops – fewer weeds could result in better crop yields; resistance to pesticides, so farmers can spray more pesticides to kill insect pests without damaging the crops

D $\frac{58}{158} \times 100 = 36.7\%$

B14.5

A identical, tissue, cuttings, embryo, specialised

B **a** it can create thousands of clones from one small piece of tissue; you cannot form many clones from one plant using cuttings

   b it needs to be carried out using specialist equipment in a laboratory; taking cuttings needs no specialist equipment, can be done be anyone

C **a** an embryo is formed by fertilisation either in a cow or in the lab; embryo is divided into several individual cells, each cell is grown in the lab into identical embryos; embryos are transferred into the uterus of host mothers; cloned calves are born

   b each calf was formed from the same embryo, so they have identical DNA

D **a** they can breed from the same cow many times a year to produce good quality calves

   b cloning decreases cattle biodiversity / may not agree with interfering with reproduction

B14.6

A cloning, same, uterus / womb

B the nucleus is removed from an unfertilised egg cell; at the same time, the nucleus is taken from an adult body cell, for example, a skin cell of another individual of the same species; the nucleus from the adult cell is inserted in the empty egg cell; the new egg cell is given a tiny electric shock, which stimulates it to start dividing to form embryo cells; these contain the same genetic information as the original adult; when the embryo has developed into a ball of cells, it is inserted into the womb of an adult female to continue its development; the cloned animal is born

C in embryo cloning the embryos produced will have a mix of genes from both the award-winning cow and a bull; the embryos that are produced will not be identical to the cow, and may not share her award-winning characteristics

in adult cell cloning the animal produced is a clone of an adult animal; this means the embryos will be identical to the cow, and share all her characteristics

D they would need a source of cells which might not be available; it is difficult to carry out successfully; with previous attempts clones have not been healthy; many people have ethical objections; the animals may no longer be adapted to the environment; cloning reduces variety in a population so it is less able to survive any changes in the environment that might happen in the future and they could become extinct again

B14.7

A inherited, benefits, increase, risk, designer

B **a** genes from GM organisms might spread into the wildlife (with unknown effects); it is a new science and long-term effects are unknown; possible effects of eating GM food on human health are unknown; concerns over genes from animals that someone doesn't eat for religious reasons / allergies being put into foods that they do eat (without any labelling of it)

b they have a need for the rice / will benefit from it, but people in the UK don't; they can't afford to eat more of foods that are rich in vitamin A / people in the UK can afford supplements or foods which naturally contain vitamin A

C **a** gene therapy

b any inherited disorder, e.g. cystic fibrosis or type 1 diabetes

c cut out healthy gene from human DNA; transfer into a vector, e.g. a virus; let virus infect the infected person's cells; the healthy gene will be inserted into their DNA

B14 Practice questions

01.1 a GM crop has had its genetic material changed / has a gene from another organism [1]

01.2 100 − 62 − 4 [1] = 34 [1]

01.3 bar drawn at 34% [1]

01.4 **two** from: possible effects on human health of eating GM food; [1] genes from GM organisms might spread into the wildlife; [1] people might create 'designer' children; [1] it is a new science and long-term effects are unknown [1]

02 example answer – **six** points (a mixture of similarities and differences) from: **similarities**: they both produce changes in characteristics; [1] both rely on variation in individuals; [1] both result from changes / mutations in DNA; [1] characteristics are passed onto offspring; [1] over time more individuals possess the characteristics; [1] **differences**: natural selection occurs naturally and selective breeding is carried out by humans; [1] natural selection takes longer than selective breeding; [1] natural selection selects for characteristics that are useful for survival, while selective breeding selects characteristics that are useful to humans [1]

B15.1

A Mendel, plants / pea plants, genes, DNA

B **a**

		Plant 1	
		t	t
Plant 2	T	**Tt**	**Tt**
	T	**Tt**	**Tt**

b 3 tall : 1 short

C **a** he shared his findings with other scientists / published his results

b other scientists discovered Mendel's papers and repeated his experiments; they saw chromosomes through a microscope

D **a** it took many scientists many years for each scientific breakthrough; scientists built on the work of those before them

b scientists are still discovering new evidence

B15.2

A Lamarck, Darwin, natural, variation, reproduction, environment, survive, offspring / children

B **a** a giraffe stretches its neck to reach the highest leaves; this characteristic is passed on to its offspring; each generation has a slightly longer neck

b there is evidence to support another theory / natural selection **or** there is not enough evidence to prove it

C **a** there is variation within a population of giraffes; some have slightly longer necks than others; the giraffes with longer necks can reach leaves on trees that the others cannot; they eat more food and are more likely to survive and breed; they pass on the genes for a long neck to their offspring; over many generations neck length increases

b the giraffes with longer necks are more likely win a fight and therefore more likely to breed with a female, passing on the genes for a long neck

c the process of evolution happens gradually over a long time / not within a lifetime, making it difficult to collect evidence

B15.3

A natural, belief / idea, evidence, inheritance / genetics

B to convince other scientists that his theory was correct

C **a** they are different shapes; each shape is adapted to allow the birds to eat different foods; each habitat has a different food source

b there is variation in beak shape, some are longer than others; the finches whose beaks are longest are best adapted to eating a food source on the island, so will get enough food to survive and breed; they will pass on this beak shape to their offspring

D **a** Alfred Russel Wallace was developing similar ideas and would publish them soon

b it challenged the belief that God made all the animals and plants on Earth; many felt there was insufficient evidence; Darwin could not explain the source of variation in characteristics / did not understand the mechanisms of inheritance and variation

c more evidence has been collected to support it; no other theory has been developed that explains *how* evolution happens; we now understand the mechanisms of inheritance and variation

B15.4

A Wallace, evolution, speciation, isolation, interbreeding / breeding

B **a** that it is poisonous, to warn predators not to eat it

b the frogs that had the strongest warning colourations would not be eaten; they would survive to pass on these markings to their offspring; over time, the markings would become stronger

C **a** speciation, geographical

b they can no longer interbreed (to create fertile offspring)

c they environments are slightly different on the two sides of the canyon; different characteristics are selected for during natural selection; eventually, the two populations are so different they can no longer interbreed

B15.5

A millions, rocks, decay, minerals, life, soft, geological

B **a** Charles Darwin

b they provide information about organisms that lived millions of years ago / that are extinct; this means scientists can study the similarities and differences between extinct organisms and living species

c the fossil record is incomplete because many fossils have been destroyed / not formed / not been found

C an animal dies and falls to the ground; the flesh rots, leaving the skeleton; layers of sediment build up over the skeleton; these form layers of rock; over millions of years minerals replace the bone tissue

D $10\,000 = 1 \times 10^4$; 1 billion $(1\,000\,000\,000) = 1 \times 10^9$; 100 million $= 1 \times 10^8$; 1 million $(1\,000\,000) = 1 \times 10^6$

B15.6

A fossils, extinction, species, predators

B **a** fossils of ancient crocodiles have been compared to modern crocodiles

b their environment has not changed very much, so they have not evolved by natural selection

C **a** overfishing meant that there was not enough food for the baiji; pollution entering the river meant that conditions were not suitable for the baiji; a new predator / animal that competed for the baiji's food starting living in the river; a disease killed the baiji

b there still might be baiji in the river, which were not seen during the expedition

D **a** between the 17th and 20th century, the number of extinctions in each century has increased, from 7 in the 17th century to 68 in the 20th century

b the human population has increased so more natural habitat has been destroyed/polluted

B15.7

A volcanic, asteroids / meteors, mass, dinosaurs, evidence

B **two** from: volcanic eruption; meteor / asteroid hitting the Earth; climate change

C dust was thrown up into the sky and darkened it; plants did not get enough light so died; lack of plants meant not enough food for dinosaurs

D **a** evidence W, X supports the asteroid collision theory; evidence V, Y, Z supports the decrease in temperature theory

b at the moment, there is more convincing evidence to support it compared to other theories

B15.8

A reproduce, antibiotics, MRSA, increases, doctors, expensive

B **first box** – at least one bacterium with a dot (to represent antibiotic-resistant bacteria); **second box** – the bacteria with no dots have a cross through them (to show which have been killed by the antibiotic); **third box** – all bacteria have dots in them

C more men than women died of MRSA infections; the number of deaths from MRSA increased between 1994 and 2006 and decreased between 2006 and 2010

D **person visiting a sick relative in a hospital**: use antibacterial hand gel on way into hospital and on leaving; **nurse working in a hospital**: wash hands well with antibacterial soap/gel in between examining patients; wear disposable clothing or clothing that is regularly sterilised; **GP who prescribes drugs**: only prescribe antibiotics for bacterial infections (not viral) when they are really needed; make sure the correct antibiotic is being used; **person who has been given antibiotics**: finish the whole course of antibiotics, even if they begin to feel better

B15.9

A Linnaeus, phylum, binomial, microscopes, classification

B kingdom, species

C animals can move their whole bodies from place to place (during at least one part of their life cycle) – plants cannot move their whole bodies about; the cells of plants have a cellulose cell wall – the cells of animals do not have a cell wall; plants can carry out photosynthesis to produce their own food – animals have to eat food

D **a** animal **b** *maritimus* **c** *Ursus*

B15.10

A kingdom, bacteria, trees

B left column, top to bottom: domain, bacteria, eukaryota; right column, top to bottom: archaebacteria, plants, protista

C **a** eukaryota **b** it contains a nucleus

D **a** 200 million years ago

b they all evolved from a common ancestor, that had four limbs

c humans and chimps both evolved from the same common ancestor that lived 5 million years ago

B15 Practice questions

01.1 *Sciurus* [1]
01.2 no; [1] they are different species [1]
01.3 140 000 + 2 500 000 = 2 640 000 [1]
$\frac{140\,000}{2\,640\,000} \times 100 = 5\%$ [1]
01.4 the grey squirrels eat the acorns before they are ripe [1] decreasing the amount of food for the red squirrel [1]
01.5 study an area with red squirrels and an area with grey squirrels; [1] the area / type of woodland must be the same; [1] count / record / compare / sample the number of woodland birds [1]
02.1 fossils [1]
02.2 3×10^9 [1]
02.3 the numbers are very big; [1] it is easier to write and understand them / introduces fewer mistakes [1]
02.4 there are no fossils from this time; [1] **one** reason from: early organisms were soft-bodied so did not form fossils; [1] they may have been destroyed by geological activity [1]

B16.1

A ecosystem, food, seed, interdependence, stable

B **a** community **b** abiotic
c biotic **d** ecosystem

C **a** a community where the abiotic and biotic factors stay relatively constant

b tropical rainforest / ancient woodland / coral reef

D plants produce food by photosynthesis and animals eat plants; animals pollinate plants so they can reproduce; animals eat animals; animals use plant and animal materials to build nests and shelters; plants need nutrients from animal droppings and decay; plants need carbon dioxide which animals breathe out; animals need oxygen which plants release from photosynthesis; some plants need animals for seed dispersal

B16.2

A light, mineral, carbon dioxide, biotic, food

B **a** animals – **two** from: temperature; availability of oxygen; availability of water

plants – **two** from: temperature; availability of carbon dioxide; availability of water; soil pH; mineral content of soil; light intensity; wind direction / intensity

b **two** from: competition from other organisms; disease; parasites; being eaten by animals

C **a** the population of ladybirds will decrease because they will die of the disease

b the population of aphids will increase because there are fewer ladybirds eating them

c the population of caterpillars will decrease because there are fewer ladybirds for blue tits to eat so they will eat more caterpillars

B16.3

A ecologists, biotic, population, distribution, quadrats, transect

B quadrat; $0.5 \times 0.5 = 0.25$ (m²)

C mussels were more evenly distributed up the shoreline than barnacles; there were more mussels than barnacles in the area sampled; barnacles were only found 15–20 m from the water's edge

D $\frac{1}{0.25} = 4$ quadrats in one square metre;
$4 \times 9 = 36$ barnacles

B16.4

A mate, adapted, offspring, different

B a mate, food / water, territory

C they can eat more different types of food, so don't have to compete as much for food with other animals

D **a** to attract a mate

b to mark its territory, to stop other leopards from entering it, stopping competition for food and mates

c to catch food, to outcompete other predators of rabbits

B16.5

A compete, food / glucose, water, soil, adaptations

B **a** so they can photosynthesise and make food

b so their roots can take in enough water and minerals, and their leaves can capture enough light

c to make amino acids / proteins and other molecules they need for growth

d to use for photosynthesis and keep their tissues rigid

C **a** to reach areas where there are fewer plants so it has more light shining on its leaves

b so the seeds spread (disperse) away from the parent plant and each other

c to cover more area in the soil for water uptake than other plants.

D **a** how spread out the seeds are

b height of seedlings; wet mass of seedlings

c **two** from: volume of water given to seedlings; temperature of surroundings; light intensity; amount of minerals

d the seeds that were spread out grew the most

B16.6

A adaptations, extremophiles, temperature

B **a** a cactus is a plant; it makes oxygen by photosynthesis

b water is essential for life; it is needed for cells to function and aids in the transport of other substances in multicellular organisms

c an oak tree needs light to carry out photosynthesis and produce food; a bacterial cell does not need light for any life processes

C **a** low temperature

b high salt concentration   **c** low light

D their enzymes do not denature / change shape at high temperatures; they can carry out essential reactions at high temperatures, e.g. respiration, metabolic reactions

B16.7

A structural, migration, functional

B **a** behavioural   **b** structural

c functional   **d** behavioural

e structural

C **a** large, thin ears / a large surface area to volume ratio

b fur

D **a** small surface area to volume ratio, to reduce heat loss

b reduces heat loss by sharing of body heat, trapping heat, protection from cold

B16.8

A decrease, spines, root, water

B **a** reduces surface area of the leaves so reduces water loss by evaporation; also, stops animals eating it

b to increase uptake of water

c so water is available at all times

C leaves are rolled inwards to reduce evaporation from the surface; leaves have a small surface area; hairs minimise air flow that could carry water away; the stomata are at the bottom of pits; no stomata on upper epidermis to reduce evaporation and transpiration

B16 Practice questions

01.1 gas exchange takes place through stomata; [1] contact with water would slow down the rate of gas exchange / diffusion **or** gas exchange is faster in air [1]

01.2 more (sun)light; [1] warmer / higher temperatures; [1] leading to faster rate of photosynthesis; [1] more mineral ions for amino acid / protein production [1]

02.1 15×7 [1] = 105 (m²) [1]

02.2 the results will not reflect the distribution correctly / any conclusions made will not be valid; [1] randomly place the quadrat [1] by using a random number generator to select coordinates [1]

02.3 1 [1]

02.4 $0 + 1 + 3 + 0 + 2 + 1 + 3 + 1 + 1 + 2 = 14$; $\frac{14}{10}$ [1] = 1.4 [1]

02.5 $1.4 \times 2 = 2.8$ [1]
2.8×105 [1] = 294 [1]

B17.1

A algae, producer, consumers, tertiary, predators

B **a** acacia tree / grass

b **two** from: giraffe; impala; zebra

c cheetah, leopard, lion

d e.g. grass → impala → cheetah → lion

C **a** solid line – rabbits; dashed line – foxes

b both populations go up and down (fluctuate); as fox numbers increase, the population of rabbits decreases; as the number of rabbits increases, so does the number of foxes

c when the number of foxes increases there are more predators so more rabbits are eaten; the population of rabbits will decrease; when the population of rabbits decreases there is less food for the foxes, so their population will decrease; when the population of foxes decreases fewer rabbits are eaten so their population increases; there is more food for the foxes so their population increases

B17.2

A decomposition / decay, soil, cycle, precipitated

B the bird died; decomposers broke down the dead body; mineral ions were released into the soil; plants took up mineral ions through their roots; the plants were eaten by a cow.

C they carry out decay / decomposition, which breaks down dead organisms and waste; this returns mineral ions to the soil, which plants can use for growth; it returns carbon to the atmosphere as carbon dioxide, which can be used by producers in photosynthesis; it 'cleans up' the environment

D clockwise from top right: precipitation, transpiration, evaporation, condensation

B17.3

A cycle, fuels, decay/decomposition, carbon dioxide, photosynthesis, eat

B **a** respiration   **b** feeding
c photosynthesis   **d** combustion

C clockwise from top left: combustion, photosynthesis, respiration, feeding

D the amount of carbon dioxide removed from the atmosphere by photosynthesis and the amount entering the atmosphere by respiration was the same

B17.4

A oxygen, moisture / water, optimum, compost, anaerobic, fuel

B line increases up to an optimum and then decreases

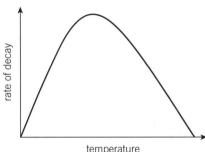

C **a** to use as a fertiliser on the garden, to increase growth of plants

b sunlight – to increase the temperature; this increases the rate of decay because chemical reactions in microorganisms are quicker so the compost is made faster
water – moisture level affects the rate of decay; microorganisms grow more quickly in moist conditions
mix – this adds oxygen into the compost so the microorganisms are able to respire aerobically and transfer energy to their surroundings, speeding up the process; without oxygen, the process does not cause a rise in temperature and is slower

D **a** the ground insulates the generator, slowing the transfer of energy from it so the contents stay warm; this increases the rate at which the biogas is produced

b to prevent too much oxygen from entering the generator to keep the process anaerobic; the reaction needs to be anaerobic so methane is made

B17 Practice questions

01.1 to show when pH becomes acidic; [1] and the reaction is complete [1]

01.2 advantage: the real reaction would take too long; [1] disadvantage: there are many other variables involved that affect the real reaction [1]

01.3 as the temperature increases the change in colour will happen more quickly; [1] the pH will decrease more quickly as fatty acids are being produced at a faster rate; [1] the activity of lipase will increase [1]

02.1 to be broken down / digested [1] by bacteria / fungi / microorganisms [1]

02.2 less oxygen available [1] for decomposers (respiration) [1]

02.3 (dead plants) / humus, then earthworm, then thrush, then hawk; [1] arrows going from left to right [1]

B18.1

A biodiversity, waste, high, reducing / decreasing, increasing, resources

B it contains a wide variety of different organisms

C **a** decrease in biodiversity; there is now only one species of tree; also, this limits the number of different animal species that can live in the forest, as not all will be able to survive with just the oil palms as a source of food / shelter

b decrease in biodiversity; insect species will be killed; also, populations of animals that eat the insects will decrease as they will have no food

D **a** 3 billion

b it will continue to increase

c we don't know what will happen in the future; the population is currently increasing but this increase may not continue at the same rate due to events that we can't predict

B18.2

A chemicals, water, fertilisers, reduce / decrease

B **a** answer between 40 and 50 m

b the concentration of oxygen and pH of the water is low; there would be fewer organisms able to tolerate these conditions, the biodiversity would be lower

C algae and water plants grow rapidly; lots of plants and algae die as they can't access the light and so can't photosynthesise; microorganisms decay the dead plants using oxygen for respiration; oxygen levels fall – animals in the pond cannot survive

D **a** **Y** – the oxygen level is high, so organisms have oxygen to respire

b **Z** – the nitrate level is high; nitrates are present in fertilisers

c **Z** – the oxygen levels are low, so most species cannot survive

B18.3

A air / atmosphere, fuels, rain, dimming

B **a** smog **b** particulates **c** fossil

C **a** **China**: sulfur dioxide emissions increase (from around 4 billion tonnes of sulfur to 16 billion tonnes); **UK**: sulfur emissions decrease (from around 2 billion tonnes of sulfur to less than 1 billion tonnes)

b **China**: it is developing very quickly, many new industries have been set up, few measures to decrease emissions; **UK**: strict emission levels were set, use of low-sulfur fuels, more electricity generated by nuclear power, flue gases from power stations cleaned

c sulfur dioxide can cause serious breathing problems; causes smog when mixed with smoke; dissolves in rainwater and reacts with oxygen in the air to form dilute sulfuric acid which falls as acid rain; acid rain can kill plants and makes lakes, rivers, and streams acidic; if the concentration of acid gets too high, plants and animals can no longer survive

B18.4

A trees, decayed, reduces / decreases, carbon dioxide

B **a** fewer trees to remove carbon dioxide from the atmosphere; trees are burnt, which releases carbon dioxide

b to increase the amount of land for farming; to build new roads / homes; to supply wood for building

C **a** $4\,100\,000 - 3\,331\,065 = 768\,935$ (km²)

b $\dfrac{768\,935}{4\,100\,000} \times 100 = 18.75\%$

D **a** it contains mineral ions

b peat is not removed from peat bogs / lands; it is important to conserve peat bogs because they act as a carbon store, removing carbon dioxide from the atmosphere; they are home to a high biodiversity of organisms; removal of peat leads to the loss of these organisms

c **one** from: the cost of each compost; the concentration and type of minerals in each compost; the pH of each compost

B18.5

A methane, warming, sea, migration

B **a** the amount of carbon dioxide in the atmosphere has increased between 1950 and 2010

b the human population has increased; so more fossil fuels are being burnt in vehicles / power stations and carbon dioxide is released; trees are being cut down (deforestation) to provide land for farming and homes, so less carbon dioxide is being removed from the atmosphere

C energy from the Sun is transferred to Earth; greenhouse gases in the atmosphere absorb some of the energy; an increase in the amount of greenhouse gases in the atmosphere increases the amount of energy absorbed; this causes an increase in average global temperatures

D **a** the climate change may make conditions more favourable for some species so they may be able to extend their range / migrate into the UK from other parts of Europe; the rate of photosynthesis will increase, causing increased growth of plants and therefore more food for insects

b low-lying areas flood by rising sea-levels, so some habitats are lost; climate change makes the UK climate less suitable for some species, e.g. too hot / cold / wet

B18.6

A water, distribution, human

B three from: soil pH, water availability, nutrients in soil, soil structure

C **a** they can only grow in habitats were the conditions are suitable

b humans are digging up peat from peat bogs, reducing the number of suitable habitats

D climate change is making more northern regions of Europe warmer; the birds will migrate to more northerly areas, as southern areas will now be too warm; there will be a higher population of birds in more northern areas

B18.7

A breeding, hedgerows, resources

B **a** **one** from: zoos educate the public about species loss; zoos may be the only protected habitat for some animals; breeding programmes increase the population of endangered animals

b **one** from: animals are kept in captivity; inbreeding may occur; captive animals may not be able to be released back into the wild

C **a** to build landfill sites large areas of land have to be cleared which could be a habitat to many plants and animals; chemicals can leak out of the rubbish and enter the land or waterways causing pollution and further loss of organisms

b recycle more; reuse items, e.g. plastic bags; buy items which have less packaging; put organic waste into a compost bin

D between 2004 and 2010, the landfill tax rose from around £18/tonne to £50/tonne; between the same years, the amount of rubbish going to landfill decreased from around 8 million tonnes to 5 million tonnes

B18.8

A trophic, producers, chain, pyramids

B by organisms eating the organisms below them in the food chain

C **a** measure the mass after removing all water / drying out the organisms

b it kills the organisms

c it decreases as you go up each trophic level

D bars should be the correct width e.g. using a scale of one small square = 100 kg; phytoplankton – 12 large (5 × 5) squares wide, small fish – 6 small squares wide; cormorant – between a single line and a maximum of 1 small square side; bars are labelled with the name of the organism; *it does not matter what the heights of the horizontal bars are*

B18.9

A algae, sunlight / light, 10, respiration, energy

B **a** it uses light energy to react carbon dioxide and water to produce glucose during photosynthesis; glucose is used to build biomass

b $500 \times \dfrac{10}{100} = 50\,g$

C **a** the cow does not digest all its food (grass); it is high in cellulose

b the cow carries out respiration at a faster rate because it needs more energy for movement and it needs to control its body temperature

c trout, because more of the biomass in the food it eats is used for growth

D they break down the biomass that is passed out as waste, and they digest the dead bodies of plants and animals

B18.10

A balanced, birth, pests, conflict

B **a** food security is having enough food to feed a population; malnutrition is a condition caused by not eating a balanced diet; sustainable food production is producing food in ways that supply the whole human population now and for future generations

b By using sustainable food production we can increase food security and decrease the risk of people suffering from malnutrition. *accept any correct sentence*

C it is linked to increasing the number of droughts and floods; these decrease the amount of food that can be grown

D Ghana, because the birth rate is much higher than the death rate; this is causing an increase in population; if food production does not also increase, there will not be enough food to feed everyone a balanced diet

B18.11

A energy, environment, movement, temperature, protein

B land that is suitable for growing crops is limited; if this land is used to grow crops for animals to graze and humans eat the animals, biomass is lost at two levels in the food chain; if humans eat crops directly then less biomass is lost; reducing the number of stages in food chains increases the efficiency of food production; there will be a greater mass of food for humans to eat

C **a** movement: so that they don't use their muscles much; this reduces the need for respiration and so they have more biomass available from their food for growth
temperature: so that the animals do not have to use much biomass in respiration for keeping warm or cooling down; this leaves more biomass for growth

b advantage: chickens grow quicker, more sold for meat in a certain time period; the farmer makes more profit
disadvantage: chickens at more risk of disease, money needs to be spent on treatment / chickens may die; they need constant monitoring which costs money

c the animals live unnatural and restricted lives / antibiotics are used routinely as a preventative rather than a cure which could be contributing to the rise in antibiotic-resistant bacteria

D the advantages of farming fish are specially bred for fast growth; they provide a cheap source of protein for people; it helps protect wild fish stocks; however, the fish are fed high-protein food that may be made from ground up wild-caught fish or cereals that could have been used for human food; some people think it is unethical to keep fish in cages and restrict their movement

B18.12

A fish, biotechnology, fungus / fungi, mycoprotein

B **a** the number of cod decrease; they were overfished, too many fish were taken from the sea so breeding could not occur successfully

b they increased; the trend on the graph from 1999 to 2002 is increasing so this trend may have continued

C **a** **one** from: controlling the size of the holes in the nets so only the biggest fish are caught; younger, smaller fish can get through the nets and live to grow large enough to breed; bans on fishing in the breeding season so fish are able to breed; strict quotas so fishermen have a limit on the amount and type of fish they are allowed to catch, allowing endangered species to recover

b it decreases the amount of fish they catch, reducing their wages; they may not agree that the methods used work to increase fish stocks

D **a** **glucose syrup** is a food source for the fungus; **pH probe** is to measure the pH – if the pH is too high or too low, the enzymes are denatured, preventing the growth of fungus; **oxygen** is needed because the fungus respires aerobically so oxygen is needed to release energy for growth

b it can be grown using cheap food sources from waste starch (which would not be used for food for humans); the fungus grows very quickly so a lot can be produced in a short amount of time; the fermenters take up less space than farms; they do not produce much pollution

B18 Practice questions

01 acid rain: sulfur dioxide / nitrogen oxides; [1] global warming: carbon dioxide / methane [1]

02.1 as the global average surface temperature rises, so does the global average sea level [1]

02.2 the rise in temperatures causes the polar ice caps to melt, [1] so there is more water in the oceans [1]

02.3 low-lying areas are at risk of flooding, [1] reducing biodiversity, [1] because fewer organisms can live in this changed habitat [1]

03.1 **four** from: place each dish in an area with the same light intensity; [1] place each dish in an area with the same temperature; [1] give each dish the same volume of water / acid; [1] use more than three seeds in each dish; [1] make sure the seeds are spread out [1]

03.2 all points plotted correctly; [2; 1 if 1 or 2 incorrect] line of best fit drawn [1]

03.3 yes, [1] because as the concentration of acid increased, the percentage of seeds that had germinated decreased [1]